On the Cusp

Where change and uncertainty are the defining elements
Where the moon moves from dark to light
A place where I have always been

A memoir

By

Margaret Gosley

Library of Congress Control Number:		2017917771
ISBN:	Hardcover	978-1-5434-8804-3
	Softcover	978-1-5434-8803-6
	eBook	978-1-5434-8802-9

Print information available on the last page.

Rev. date: 12/06/2017

To order additional copies of this book, contact:
Xlibris
800-056-3182
www.Xlibrispublishing.co.uk
Orders@Xlibrispublishing.co.uk
770464

Contents

To Shoshannah, Robin and Natty
With all my love

PROLOGUE

I came into this world at a time of great uncertainty; conceived in the early months of 1939, I was born in the November of that year just two months after the outbreak of World War II. So I am of the generation that stands astride two very different times. I was formed and brought up to the values of the rigidly conforming fifties. But I became an adult throughout the creative and liberating years of the sixties. I also came to have two sets of parents, one genetic and one adopted and for an adopted child both sets of parents are important. Even if you never know the first set, maybe never even care to know them, never give them a second thought, they live within you. They are stitched into the fabric of your being.

My genetic father does not loom large in this story. I met him only once and he seemed a domineering presence although there must have been more to him than that. In a photograph that I have of him he looks arrogant and I am told he was a clever man. But then fathers can so often be difficult. I battled with my adopted father throughout my life but it was him who allowed me to talk, to dissect my life and my politics. We frequently fell out over values and ideas but he was always there to love me and provide for me.

My adopted mother took me in because she loved me. She loved and nurtured me however difficult I was and she is responsible for all the best bits in me. Through her and her love I learnt to withhold judgement, accept people for what they are and expect the good in them. I have always felt that my later socialist values lay with her upbringing. She was so careful for me to know that I was as equally loved as her two natural daughters and went to great lengths to demonstrate it. She once told me, with the best and most loving of intentions, that when she was giving her medical history to a new doctor, she told him she'd had three pregnancies. She quite forgot that she had not actually given birth to me, her middle daughter whom she'd adopted as a tiny baby. She would have been heartbroken to have known that instead of reassuring me it raised troubling questions for me. If it was so easy to forget whether or not one had given birth, I asked myself, what meaning or value did the blood tie have, and how important were all those myths of birthing and bonding? What value was there in those early hours of parenthood if there could be such an easy confusion over remembering and forgetting? My mother's story was well meant but turned my world into a shifting place with everything depending upon a forgotten moment. Of course she did not mean to have this result with the telling of this story. For her it was proof positive of how much she loved her middle daughter but for me it raised yet another uncertainty. She told me the story because she wanted me to have proof that I was loved the same as my sisters. It was her gift to me but the very telling of it set me apart. Why did I have to be given proof of my parents love when my sisters didn't? Not for one minute do I doubt my Mother's love for me and mine for her. But through no fault of hers there was always this shadow of uncertainty within me and always this feeling of being set apart. I hope I have done my Mother's love justice and grown up as her example. But the doubts are there and as I come to know a little more about my genes I find that nature is in there along with nurture.

My nurturing parents described my genetic mother to me as small with dark hair and pretty. They did not tell me I looked like her but said I had eyes like hers. Through my personal search for my origins and the paper evidence of birth and marriage certificates I learnt more about the bare facts of her life. I met her twice, once when I was a young woman and once in my middle age. The meetings were brief and yes, I did look like her. I also discovered she had a creative side to her nature and most importantly, just like me, she had kept written notebooks throughout her life. The second time I met her I was in my fifties and she an old lady. We sat side by side on her sofa in her bungalow and she showed me a shoebox full of what she called her 'scribblings'. Over and over again she had written out her pain, her feelings of shame and loneliness on scraps of paper and in cheap notebooks. To this day I wonder if this is something you can inherit since writing things down is also how I deal with things. Not in any order or a journal, just notebooks written under the pressure of need. I see now that they are the way in which I constructed a narrative that would legitimise me and provide me with a history.

At the age of ninety and at my request my birth mother sent me her 'scribblings'. The narrative of her brief life with me came through the post in a large brown envelope. As I gently drew them out of the envelope a smell hit the back of my nose, a blow that pushed me back and forced me to sit down. To say the smell was familiar is not sufficient or even true because I could not match it to anything I consciously remembered. But it was not unfamiliar in the sense that it felt like me and it made me cry. Sitting, crying, with these 'scribblings' on my lap I could not read them until many days later but I was haunted by the smell of them. When I finally read them, my birth mother and her pain became very real for me. She had been able to have and to hold me for at least the first six weeks of my life. Did she breathe in my baby smell before she gave me away? And did the smell of her linger in my nose before it travelled to that part of the brain that records and locks away our memories until something sets them free. My birth mother's 'scribblings' had a profound effect upon me and I am lucky to have them. It is through them that I am able to honour her side of the story.

If you are an adopted child, however smooth and happy that process may have been; however loved you were within your family, you learn to perform with a fine precision and develop a heightened sense of what is required in order to be accepted as a proper person. I also suspect that the parents of the adopted child must always have that sliver of fear; a fear of the part of you they do not know and cannot guess at as they seek to bring you up in the best and most loving way. Your genetic heritage is there, lurking in the wings and despite all their best love and parenting efforts may yet strike and take them by surprise.

The adopted child is someone from outside the mould and lives as an exile in a foreign land. It has affected my life with questions such as Who am I? Where do I belong? How should I behave? As far as knowing who I truly was, I always felt I stood on the edge of a black hole that contained my past, my inherited self. As to how I should behave, I had my parents there for guidance but did not know how that unknown past might inform the future. All that was in the dark hole behind me so it was up to me to constantly invent myself.

As a child I wanted to fit the mould but I was never too sure what it was nor, since I was desperately unsure as to who I was, whether the mould fitted me. I frequently failed and failure made me resent the mould, made me angry with it. To protect myself from my own failure I constantly challenged it and at the same time removed myself to the edge of things where I felt safe and at home. Later in life this became a kind of modus operandi yet it was never entirely self-conscious. I admit that I have used this sense of being an outsider as an excuse for failure. If I had tried a bit harder I might have succeeded in being a more regular and successful person. I don't want to sound sorry for myself because I am not. I just want to show how the circumstances of our beginnings can inform and underpin the rest of our lives

1

The Beginning

My genetic mother's name was Mildred and she gave birth to me on the bedroom floor of a small terraced house that was her grandparents' home in North Yorkshire. She has since told me that she 'can never forget that blue lino'. She herself was born in Sutton-in-Ashfield, Nottinghamshire, where she and her sister lived in rented rooms with their mother, who was always ill and father, who was a journeyman miner. They were very poor and eventually her mother died of pernicious anaemia for which at that time there was no cure. When her Father remarried, his daughters, as in a proper fairy story, were not welcome and he left them with their grandparents in Helmsley, Yorks. They were taken in grudgingly and it was made clear to Mildred that she would have to contribute to her living. She left school at the age of fourteen to work in a local hairdressers until she went into service as a live-in nanny with various families. She describes how she met my father Hal at a dancing class when she was only eighteen:

> *Mildred's scribblings*
>
> *We were two naïve innocents, two people searching for someone to care as it transpired that Hal was not living at home having fallen out with his parents and gone to live in lodgings. We were more companions than lovers for many months but we began to feel deeply for each other although the word 'love' was never mentioned. We were totally naïve but knew that if we were to take our love any further we had to take precautions.*
>
> *What a fiasco! which ended with the accident happening. The very thing we knew we must avoid.*

> *To say that the next few weeks were worrying is an understatement. But strangely enough the very fact that for the first time in my life I had someone to care for me gave me the feeling that come what may we would be able to cope somehow.*

But they were not able to cope, circumstances were going to make sure of that. And they had nothing in the way of support. Hal's mother was a strict Irish catholic who banished him and refused to recognise the pregnancy. The War was imminent and Hal had to either join the army or, as he was an industrial chemist, go South to work on the armaments at the Woolwich Arsena; unsurprisingly he chose to go South. Since the pregnancy was illegitimate Mildred's grandparent's declared her to be evil and sent her to a home for 'fallen women' which was run by the Church Army in Harrogate. However the grandparents or possibly it was Hal's parents, were adamant that she and Hal had to be married although quite why we shall never know and they never gave them any further support in the future. So in the September of 1939 the two of them met to be married at York Registry office:

> *The ultimation had been issued. Hal and I were to be married whether we wanted to or not. Neither of us had been involved in any of the discussions, arguments, threats and the subsequent bad feelings between the two families. They never spoke to each other again.*
>
> *A wedding day was arranged for us in a registry office in York. What a day! I honestly would not have blamed Hal if he had run a mile such was the atmosphere of hate through all this. I think that had we been able to contact each other we might both have run away.*
>
> *I was collected from the 'Home for Fallen Women' in the morning. Previously my own grandmother had, with thought and understanding sent me a small amount of money to buy something decent to wear for the occasion. As the Church Army Officials opened all the letters sent to the Home this was confiscated. I do not know what became of the money. I was just told that as I had sinned it was a part of my punishment and they would give it to a good cause.*
>
> *I was the first to arrive in this grim little room at the Registry Office. Nearby stood my grandparents who stood in stoney silence. Hal's parents did not attend as they had disowned him and when he arrived we dare not look at each other. If only we had been able to comfort and support each other just then! We just solemnly made*

our wedding vows. We were not even allowed to say good-bye to each other. I was bundled into the car back to Harrogate and Hal went back to London where he now worked. We were not to see each other again until the birth of our child, Margaret in November and then only for one afternoon. It was then that we both somehow knew that come what may we would find a way of being together again. And we did but even fifty years later we have never been able to talk about this terrible time in our lives.

For Mildred there was worse to come. War had been declared and the Church Army Officials were required to close down the Home in Harrogate as the staff and the premises were needed for the war effort. The 'fallen women' were given two weeks to make other arrangements and Mildred according to her notes, had nowhere else to go but back to her grandparents:

Now began a most difficult time in my life. Grandfather pretended I did not exist and totally ignored me. My Grandma, a kindly, simple lady, did her best under difficult circumstances to make life easier. On a few occasions I heard her taking him to task for treating me, in her own words, 'worse than a pig'.

I knew absolutely nothing of what to expect about having a baby. It was a taboo subject. Indeed all the time I was at my grandparents I was never able to go outside unless after dark because of the shame I had brought to the family. Oh how I wished I had a loving, understanding mum who would put an arm around my shoulder. But I had learnt by this time never to cry whatever happened.

Although they describe a really dreadful time and I find it very hard to read Mildred's scribblings, at this point I also feel very privileged to have her words for she was after all the truest witness to the first and one of the very few experiences we shared:

The day Margaret was born, this child of shame, I had no medical help of any kind and such was the agony that I vowed never again! In the early hours of the morning I lit a candle and found shoes and coat to go to the toilet or 'lav' as it was usually called. A wet cold, windy walk in the dark up the cinder path in the garden. There was no fancy flush toilet here. But for the fact that there was no running water it looked quite palatial. The wooden top being made of what must have been a very nice carved oak bedstead with the appropriate hole cut into it. The rain drumming on the tin roof and the wind making the candle flicker made it all seem very surreal.

I, in my total ignorance knew absolutely nothing about what to expect but dimly realised that I felt very uncomfortable. Not in pain yet, that in all its vengeance was to come a few hours later. I almost felt the hours of agony were the price I had to pay for my wickedness. Kneeling on the cold lino covered floor in the bitter cold bedroom daylight arrived with the sound of the fire being lit in the kitchen below. At no time had I ever had any medical attention, probably the cost would have been too high, no NHS then.

The rest of the day fear, cold, indescribable agony as relentlessly the hours passed until in the evening in candlelight Margaret was born. A pretty, dark haired moppet. I couldn't help wondering how we were going to cope, what life had in store for you. It was always made very plain to Hal and me that we were sinners and I hoped that the old saying about 'the sins of the father's being visited on the children' would not apply to you. I wrote to Hal who immediately came up from London. I was ashamed of the way he was treated. He spent the day upstairs with me and the baby. My grandparents barely spoke to him and never even offered him a cup of tea. Small wonder that he couldn't wait until it was time to go and he forever hated them.

So followed a most unhappy time. I was left in no doubt by the old chap that we were nothing but a nuisance. I was terrified in case Margaret cried at night and spent many cold nights walking and rocking to keep her quiet all night as I was constantly reminded what a bloody burden I was. I knew there would be difficult decisions to be made and I hoped I would be able to do the right thing.

But Hal was in London which was by now being regularly bombed and Mildred had a new born baby and no support. Who amongst us would know what the 'right thing' was?

Hal had found us a bed-sit in Plumstead. I didn't know how we were going to manage but in desperation decided I must go. Hal came for me so we struggled onto the train at York in the black out. The train was full of troops and we felt so lost and vulnerable.

Out of the blue and before I left my grandparents I had a letter from the family that I had previously worked for as their nanny. They said they had some friends who would be willing to foster our

*baby. As they lived outside of London and away from the bombing
they thought it would be a good thing to let Margaret go to them.*

*We had an agonizing night of indecision and all night I could
not stop cuddling Margaret. We dreaded that it would be the next
thing to do. We went to see this couple and were in no doubt how
genuine they were. So we left Margaret in a good loving home
but never have I felt such emptiness. I used to wake up at night
imagining I could hear her cries and I could actually smell that
scented baby smell. It felt like the torment would never end.*

My newfound mother whose name was Olive did describe to me how
Mildred and Hal used to come and visit me on some Sunday's. She told me how
she used to brush my hair and put me in my prettiest clothes for them. They
would take me out in the pram for a walk and presumably to have some time
alone with me. My mother/Olive tells me how horribly jealous she increasingly
became; how anxious she used to feel and then so guilty for feeling that way.
So, in my pretty dress and brushed hair I was the focal point for a great deal
of anxiety and stress on all sides:

*I had to find work and Hal worked long, arduous hours.
We had air raids, bombs, the black out, and all the trials of war.
Because of the restricted transport we were unable to have time off
work and unable to see Margaret very often. So the weeks went into
months and the months into years but the emptiness never left me.*

After two years, while the War still continued, my newfound father
Charles decided that he had to do something. He wrote to Mildred and Hal
telling them that I was starting to talk and calling them mummy and daddy.
Moreover they loved me and and were finding the thought of giving me up
increasingly difficult. So they needed Mildred and Hal to make a decision
about my future:

*We then had a letter from the young couple who were her foster
parents. It said they had grown to love her and thought of her as
their own. She was also calling them mummy and daddy and the
time had come to ask us to let them adopt her. If not they would
have to reluctantly ask us to come and take her away before she got
any older and it had to be explained that they were not parents.*

*There then began an agonizing few weeks which was very
distressing for both of us. We decided rightly or wrongly that we
could not in the circumstances justify dragging Margaret from a*

comfortable, loving home to what we, as by now virtual strangers, could offer her. So with heavy hearts we gave her up hoping that one day she might understand and try to forgive us.

So there I was having safely made the journey from dark to light. Though of course the dark side always lurked there as a cloud of uncertainty.

2

Growing Up

I was not officially adopted until 1941 so for the first two years of my life I appear to have been betwixt and between. I had the good fortune however to fall into the lap of a family who not only loved me but wanted to keep me as well. Olive and Charles, who had come to love me enough to want to become my legal parents, lived in what was then the small village of Great Gadsden just outside Hemel Hempstead in Hertfordshire. They already had a four year old daughter who became my eldest sister. She has told me that she remembers my coming home and that I had lots of dark hair. My newfound parents were always happy for me to know and to talk about my origins but we talked very little about those first two years when I belonged yet didn't quite belong. I always wanted to know more about how they felt but was too shy to ask just in case they thought I was being disloyal and they would stop loving me.

In this I completely under estimated the unconditional love that my new parents had for me. I had a very happy childhood which is not to say that I was not difficult; always testing the boundaries, looking for the limits of love. All children do it as part of growing up but I tested it constantly and at every level. One of my big battles with my parents was over the eating of cabbage which I hated. When I refused to eat it which I did regularly at the Sunday dinner table my temper would often explode and I was sent out into the hallway to 'quieten down and come back when you can behave'. I would sit on the stairs filled with fury and a great hatred of cabbage which, since I have left home, I have never eaten.

This hallway is where I place my memories of encountering the smell of my family. Every home has its own smell but those who belong to it are not aware of it. They are born of it; they create it; it comes off their bodies. It is how animals know which pack they belong to because the wrong pack doesn't smell right. In the hallway I always smelt my family smell and the fact that I could smell it meant I didn't smell the same. This made me feel ugly and dirty and not a 'right' person. I was loved and nurtured all my life by my family but because of my smell I never quite felt legitimate. My nose knew that I was not a true member of the pack.

Whenever I had been naughty my mother always found a way of helping me back into the family circle and more often than not comforted me with the words 'you are very special to us because we didn't just have you, we chose you'. I can remember sitting in the hallway full of not only fury but fear as well that this might be the moment when they chose not to love me. Although I was undoubtedly loved being chosen to be loved is more dangerous. There is nothing certain or absolute about choice. It isn't like blood or genes. However bad or naughty my sisters might be they could not undo that genetic knot that tied them to my parents. They could not stop being my parents children, it was fixed in blood whereas I could be un-chosen at any moment. Of course I never was and my mother always found a way to help me back into the family circle. But it also created in me a self-imposed necessity to try and be not just good, but the right kind of person that fitted in well enough to remain chosen. All children try to be good and fail at times but for me the need was so filled with anxiety that when I failed to be good or get it right it was always as if some real, unknown me was exposed and unlovable. My only self defense was to reject and run away from what was required.

The hallway in a house is the entrance to the home life within but it also sits just outside of the family life. For me to be just outside of things remains the place where I feel most secure because it is a place where I can't do anything wrong. This feeling or need has under-pinned my whole life. It has been a constant source of anxiety and affected all my relationships. I never quite trusted that the dark uncertainties of my beginnings might not be rooted in my genes; that I might be found out or give myself away at any time. I tried hard to be a good girl but the effort of it frequently made me a naughty girl.

As a child I loved playing out on the front street where we children all played since there were very few cars about, and I invariably made a scene when my mother called me in. It happened regularly and was one of those times when I regularly failed to get it right and be a good girl. Rather than wait to be chosen I would run away. I used to run round the block, my heart beating with the humiliation of getting it wrong. Then when my anger with myself subsided and I realised I had nowhere else to go I would trail home. My Mother was such a wise and loving woman. She would be waiting for me and my running away was never mentioned. She simply dried my tears, enfolded me in her love and steered me back into the heart of the family.

Four years after my parents adopted me they had another child, a daughter of their own. It was 1945, the war had ended and times were set to be more certain. I now became the middle child lodged securely between my two sisters. We moved to a little semi-detached house in North Watford which my parents initially rented and were later able to buy as my father's work situation improved. It was on a small estate of identical houses all of which had gardens which backed onto the houses of the next street but were separated by a back ally. At one time during the war we also had two evacuee boys living with us who we came to think of as our cousins and I have always wondered how we all fitted into that little house. I do remember that on warm, sunny evenings when I was about four years old my older sister and the two boys used to get me to call out rude words like 'bottom' from the back bedroom window so that they floated into the next door garden. They would scream with laughter and even though we got told off I always felt immensely proud of the pleasure I felt I had given them.

My Mother was a qualified nursery nurse and my earliest memory is of going to nursery with her on the back of her bike. She worked in the baby room but I was in the toddler room. My agony here was that we had to lie down every afternoon on little fold up canvas beds for an afternoon rest. I dreaded the boredom of this as I had far too much energy to be able to sleep. What saved the day for me was that we each had a small quilt to cover us which had apparently been donated by the American Air Force. They were covered with material printed with pictures from various fairy tales which meant I could lie and 'read' my quilt through the rest hour. At the end of the day I had to go to the baby room and sit quietly to wait for my mother. The room was full of cots and had two windows with a baby doll sitting on each window sill. They were fully dressed in hand knitted matinee coats, bonnet and boots, one in pink and one in blue. I longed to play with them as I waited for my mother but they were only for show and not for touching.

My father was not an easy man but he worked hard to provide for us and keep us safe. He had not had a happy childhood himself since his father died when he was young. His mother did not have the means to keep all her four children so my father was put out to live with an uncle. He had to leave school when he was fourteen to work on a local farm, presumably to help pay his way and he showed us how he could not move his big toe because he had to wear boots that did not fit him. He told us how the coldest he had ever been was pulling up carrots, on a cold frosty morning before the sun was fully up. But despite this hardship it was always his dream to have a small holding of his own. He never fulfilled that dream but lived it out in the succession of gardens to our childhood homes.

The back garden of my early childhood was quite long and my father kept both chickens and rabbits down the end of it. The eggs and the rabbits presumably filled out our war time diet. I remember my father cleaning out and preparing a rabbit. The smell was horrible but I hung around so my father could give me a lucky dead rabbit's foot. One day in August my sister and I were both sent to our next door neighbours for the day. This was a great treat because we had plums and custard for pudding. We were back in the garden and my father had just collected the eggs from his chickens when the news came from the mid-wife shouting from the window, that the new baby had arrived safely and was a girl. My eldest sister's most vivid memory of this day is that my father said 'damn!' because one of the eggs was cracked and he threw it to the ground. I find it interesting that my sister remembers that day of our younger sister's birth with the egg incident and I remember the plums and custard!

If the garden was an expression of where my father's heart lay it was also one of the places where he provided fun and great happiness for myself and my two sisters. One of my favourite things was the swing which my Father built for us and we were the only kids in the street to have one. It had really thick, strong ropes and a wooden seat that was not much more than a plank but had been smoothed and was very warm and comfy. A consistent feature in my memory of my father is that he would regularly return from the distant world of 'going to work' with stuff that he had acquired in some way that always remained a mystery to us all at home. The rope was one such example and was considered excellent and special by the grown ups. Since it was built by my father it was not just any old swing but had to be a top ranking one. I remember adult conversations about the special bearings that my father had been so clever to use so that the swing would truly swing. And indeed it did. I spent hours swinging and singing on it as I suspect my sisters did too. There is a faded black and white photo taken with my parents' Brownie box camera, bought with the help of Kensitas cigarette coupons, of me hanging upside down between its splendid ropes, my pigtails sweeping its seat.

To one side and a few yards away from the swing was a lilac tree that in spring filled with sweet smelling purple blossoms. My trick was to swing higher and higher, kicking my legs out in front of me until I was almost level with the top of the lilac tree. Then on the cusp of the upward flight I let go of the ropes and leapt off the swing for one glorious moment of flying through the air, free from every trouble and constraint along with a thrilling lurch in the stomach just before I hit the ground. I could calculate the exact moment to make the jump so that I could have the thrill without coming to harm. Handstands and cartwheels were also my forte and another way of getting that rush that comes with freeing oneself from the grip of gravity followed by the feeling of empowerment that comes through your ability to control the landing.

At the very bottom of the garden was the garage which was built on a slightly sunken area that had once housed the Anderson shelter during the war. We had only ever used this shelter once during the war when my grandmother came to stay. She was terrified of the doodle bombs and in the middle of the night that she stayed with us, at her insistence, we were all herded into the shelter. I remember being carried down the garden in my father's arms and being very proud that I was wearing my sister's dressing gown. The floor of the shelter was earthy and there were two crude bunk beds on either side. I was sat with my eldest sister on one of them and she scared me by telling me that there were earwigs out to get me. We were perfectly safe since my father reckoned he had worked out the angle of flight for any passing German bomber and built the shelter where it couldn't possibly be hit. And if course it wasn't although a single bomb did drop not that far from us. We went with my father to see the hole and there was a boy there stretching a great bulge in his jumper as he filled it up with bits of shrapnel.

When my father first came South from his Uncle's farm in Yorkshire it was to work as a chauffeur for a wealthy family who owned a machine tool company. They trained my father as an engineer and turner in order to work on repairing the lathes and milling machines that they sold. This was a protected occupation so my father did not have to go to the war. But he was in the Home Guard and I remember being afraid of the heavy, dark green, great coat that hung on the back of the kitchen door. My father was obviously good at his job and rose up the ranks of the firm so that by the end of the war my parents could afford to buy the house they rented and the Anderson shelter was demolished to make way for a garage and our newly acquired, second hand Austin Seven.

I never liked this car nor any car come to that as I was dreadfully travel sick as a child and this was before the days of travel pills. When we drove to visit my grandmother in Norfolk I would be sick several times on the way. So by the time we arrived I was always ravenously hungry and remember my grandmother's fish cakes with relish. Drives into the countryside were a leisure pursuit for us on a Sunday and I hated them, not just because of the travel sickness but because they were so boring. I can remember looking out of the window at passing woodlands. They looked perfect places for playing and I couldn't understand why we couldn't stop and do just that. But this was not my father's mission and the drive went on and on. Sitting in the back seat between my two sisters I grew bored and would start to torment them with little nips to their arms and bottoms. My eldest sister fought back as our youngest sister's complaints grew louder. Finally my father would pull up and tell me that if I didn't stop he would put me out. I cried and for the rest of the journey I knelt up with my back to the family and stared out of the back window. I hoped that people would see me and think that I was a cruelly captured princess.

It was around this time in my early childhood that my father brought home a large box of dressing up clothes given to him by the people he worked for. These were not grown-ups cast offs but genuine costumes. They were the kind of things you might wear to a fancy dress party and they provoked a spell of performing in my sister and her friends. The garage became a theatre with curtains opening out onto the back alley. The audience of kids from the rest of the street sat on a roughly fashioned bench to watch my sister and her friend singing and flouncing in the wonderful dressing up costumes. I was the person allocated to opening and closing the curtains which I was very bitter about since I knew that I was the great performer in the family. All children have to learn how to fit in with the family, the school, the group, it is a part of growing up but it had a particular importance in my life. My family had always been keen for me to know the circumstances of my beginnings and I cannot remember not knowing that I was adopted.

We always talked openly about it as a family and I was always free to ask questions and express my feelings. But some of them were too difficult because they made me feel guilty and like a traitor if I spoke them out loud. It seemed to me that I was born one person but I had to become another. I felt I had to learn the subtle signs of what was required and perform in order to keep my place as a daughter in this family. This pressure did not come from my family who loved me without question, but from my birth family who had abandoned me. I felt that I was loved when I got it right and not unloved but without a self when I got it wrong. This loss of self made me explode with anger and I must have been a difficult child. I can still hear my father saying 'sometimes I think you would be happier if we had never told you' And therein lies a truth I think. My father could have been right all along. It may be the knowing of things that is as meaningful as the actual experience of them. Certainly it meant that performance was always a part of my identity and that even as a grown up I still needed applause as reassurance that I am a proper person.

3

School

When I started school I was already a fairly proficient performer. I knew how to blend in, closely observe and court my audience until I felt sufficiently well loved to perform the appropriate self. But I didn't always get it right and sometimes my frustration at what I had to be would spill over and get me into trouble. It was perhaps not surprising that my success at school was not academic but theatrical. Maybe inheritance comes not only through our genes because there is a strong thread of theatrical performance on my adopted father's side of the family. He was always heavily involved in various amateur dramatic groups throughout my childhood and I have a strong memory of him in tights, leaning against the proscenium arch and declaiming 'If music be the food of love' etc. I also made the most of a kind of kudos it gave me. I was amongst those who stayed for school dinners which in those immediate times after the war consisted of a large enamel mug of stew filled out with dehydrated carrots and pearl barley and which I absolutely hated. We had our dinner break in the school hall where there was a small stage. This often had signs of the current amateur dramatic production that was being rehearsed there in the evenings and I bathed in the reflected glory of my father, who was not just in it, but often in the lead.

The performer in me first gained public recognition and applause when I starred in the annual school play. I have a photograph of me draped in chiffon with a tiara in my hair. I am queen of the fairies surrounded by my band of fairy followers. I can't remember the plot or even the performance except that I had a final line that was sad and wistful. Now, I have a natural and permanent crack in my voice and I must have used this to great affect because I apparently brought tears to the audience. I remember my mother hugging me close after the show as though she was almost afraid that I had escaped her grasp and it is one of the rare times when I felt my father was really proud of me. In the photograph I am leaning slightly forward and looking straight into the camera. There is an intensity in my eyes and in my body that makes me look quite adult.

The passion for acting had caught me but there was a warning in it too. Miss Roberts was my class teacher with a reputation for being very strict and she helped with the show. My mother told me that, as Miss Roberts was making up my eyebrows she said to my mother 'Margaret has lovely eyes but she likes the boys'. My mother repeated this story regularly throughout my childhood, almost like a warning. I was shocked by it because it simply wasn't true, I didn't care about boys at all. It was much later in my life that I came to realise that there is a geometry between the sexes and especially so in those days. Girls seemed to know instinctively how to position themselves in relation to boys. But I was never aware of this. I was full of energy and because of this, as a child I often played with boys because I wanted to do boys' things like climbing trees etc. I suppose I always talked with boys as an equal without knowing I was doing it.

The first time I was ever asked out by a boy I did it all wrong. This happened in about my third or fourth year at secondary school when someone started leaving notes saying 'I love you' in my desk. I ignored these and told no one about them. But it suddenly seemed that everyone was starting to 'go out' with someone and to make matters worse my best friend Shirley started walking home after school with a boy called Mick. One morning at break Shirley dragged herself away from her huddle with Mick to tell me that his best friend Anthony wanted to go out with me. I was embarrassed and definitely not interested in Anthony but over night I had second thoughts. I still didn't care about Antony but realised it would give me someone to walk home with and more importantly, it would make me fit in and be like everyone else. So the next day I approached Shirley and Mick and said "You can tell Anthony I will go out with him". It was Shirley's turn to be embarrassed now as Mick replied "Who do you think you are! You don't get asked twice you know!". I was so humiliated and vowed never to put myself through that again. It would be acting that would bring me public acclaim and success from now on.

I was the first in the family to pass the eleven plus and go to grammar school. I have always felt that it was the changing times, along with my Father's gradual climb up the ladder of social and economic success that made the difference in the experience that my two sisters and I had of the eleven plus and grammar schools. When my eldest sister took the eleven plus the war was still on; my father still worked on the factory floor; and my family still rented the housed we lived in. She did not take the exam in the familiar surroundings of her primary school but in a hall in the town along with children from many other schools. My father had to take time off and borrow a 'works' car to get her there so the experience was overlaid with the anxiety of the unfamiliar. Moreover when the letter came to tell her that she had failed to pass it also said that she was next on the list and if someone dropped out then she could have a place. Of course nobody did drop out and she consequently went to a 'secondary mod' as they were called. From there she went on to follow in our mother's footsteps and train as a nursery nurse. Unfortunately she qualified at a time when the nurseries that had been so necessary during the war were now beginning to close down. The men wanted to reclaim the jobs that the women had been doing in their absence and books like John Bowlby's Maternal Care and Mental Health promoted the need to get women back into the home and caring for their children. My sister found it hard to get a job as a nursery nurse so she retrained as a hairdresser and did not return to work as a nursery nurse until her own children were in school.

I took the eleven plus in 1951 when the times were becoming more affluent both in general and for my own family. My Father had moved over onto the management side of the firm he worked for. He was buying the house we had once rented and we owned our own car. I took the exam in the comfort of my primary school and there must have been very little pressure since I don't actually remember taking it. The pressure came after I had passed the exam because I had to have an interview to determine which grammar school I was going to. My home town had three grammar schools. There was the Grammar School for Girls and the Boys Grammar School both of which were over a hundred years old. They were very traditional and were thought of as very posh. The other grammar school was a former secondary modern school turned into a co-educational Grammar school to cope with the baby boom years after the war.

My interview took place at the Girls Grammar School and I knew it was important because my Father took the afternoon off work to drive my Mother and I there, this time in our own car. I had been sent an extract from Huckleberry Finn to prepare for reading at the interview but it must have been a school's edition since the real book is written in the vernacular. I was not questioned on the extract so presumably it was just to see how well I could read and speak. My parents and I waited in the corridor outside the dark door of the headteacher's office and when my name was called I tripped and stumbled on the door sill as I went into the office. I remember this clearly because I always thought this was why I didn't get into the Girls Grammar School; that I was just not sufficiently ladylike and so was relegated to the new Grammar school on the outskirts of town. By the time my younger sister took the eleven plus five years later, my Father had become managing director of the company he worked for. We had moved to the 'better' part of the town and lived in a large detached house built to my Father's own design. His stated ambition had always been to live in a house that did not look like all the others in the row which it most certainly didn't and not surprisingly my younger sister went to the 'posh' Girls Grammar School.

Maybe fate handed me the card I needed because the new grammar school was perfect for me. My year was the first eleven plus intake and the school badly wanted us to succeed. Many of our teachers came from that generation of men, and they were mostly men, that had seen the war, were highly educated themselves and wanted to do well by us because they wanted the world to be a better place In my third year at grammar school, which would be year nine these days, I had to make my choices for which 'O' levels I would take. This coincided with my having my teeth straightened. I had a small mouth so my front teeth were slightly crooked and pushed forward. This was in the early days of the tooth straightening business. My dentist was not equipped to do it and sent me to the Royal Dental Hospital in Leicester Square, central London. I had to have teeth pulled out to make room then braces put on to straighten them up. The braces had to be tightened at regular intervals which meant a trip to London with my mother which I loved. At one point I was even asked to go in on a particular Saturday and sit there as an example of the new procedures for some visiting Australian dentists. I was paid ten shillings for doing it which was a huge sum of money for me and I can still see that pink ten shilling note though I don't remember what I spent it on or if I was even allowed to spend it.

Although the tightening of the braces made my teeth ache, my mother and I always stopped at a cafe on the way home for tea and a cake which was another huge treat and made me feel very special. Although coffee bars were beginning to make their presence felt on the high streets neither my family nor most of the middle class in England had yet got the habit of eating and drinking out. I also loved the Royal Dental Hospital which was in a large, quite imposing and ornate building on a corner in Leicester Square. What I liked was the feeling of community through shared purpose between the people, dentists and assistants etc. who worked there. It felt safe and attractive so I decided I wanted to be a dentist and consequently opted to take two science subjects at 'O' level. This was a big mistake since I had absolutely no talent for science; failed them both and I gave up on the dentist idea. Whilst I was still in the fifth form, year ten in todays' language, the School employed a new, charismatic young French teacher called Mr Lee who also took on the task of the school theatrical productions. My moment came when he chose me to play Emily, the lead, in Thornton Wilder's play 'Our Town'. It was such a special time and we became a close and dedicated ensemble. We rehearsed after school and had the use of the domestic science room so that we could make beans on toast before starting. On the nights of big, full cast rehearsals, we would be allowed to walk to the Busy Bee lorry driver pull-in for fried egg on toast. We felt so grown up and I seemed to have spent most of that school term walking around in a bubble of special-ness.

Apparently I repeated my junior school performance in my sad and wistful closing speech. I guess my cracked voice payed off again and we brought the house down. This time the question of Margaret and the boys thing took on a reality. The Narrator in Our Town was played by a tall and handsome boy called Nobby Clarke. Off stage I rarely spoke to him because he was popular and always surrounded by girls who knew exactly how to place themselves boy/girl wise unlike myself who hadn't a clue. So I kept my distance. The line-up for the curtain call had me centre stage and flanked by the two male leads one of whom was Nobby and who by now had an almost god like aura amongst the girls. As the lights went up and we stepped forward into the applause to take our bow Nobby squeezed my hand, magic gave way to rapture and my blood fizzed like champagne.

Nobby Clarke became my first boyfriend although he was not really my type since he was a keen Boy Scout and a football player. But I adored being chosen by him. It was an extension of that glorious curtain call. Then came the night when we went on a school trip to see John Neville as Richard II at the Old Vic. I was bowled over by it; by the theatre; the poetry of the play; and John Neville who became my heart throb. We had to come home by train and my father had arranged to pick me up at the station. Nobby had been hanging out with his mates and distant with me all evening. As we waited for the train I plucked up courage, pushed my way through to him and asked him if he wanted a lift home with me and my dad. "Oh, it's OK" he said, hardly even turning towards me "I'm going back with my mates". We went home in separate train carriages and I was devastated. It was the end of our romance. The words of Richard II: 'Bury me on the king's highway since now you tread upon my heart' became my theme and from then on I stayed close to my girl friends.

The summer holiday between the fifth and sixth form, Otto Preminger announced that he was to make a film of Joan of Arc and that he was setting out to search the capitals of Europe for an unknown actress to play the part. My best friend Lesley showed me the announcement in the 'Picturegoer' magazine which she regularly read. We giggled quite a bit and then finally plucked up courage to fill in the application form and send it off. To my huge excitement an airmail letter came, an extraordinary thing in itself and even more so since it was postmarked Hollywood. Inside was a letter inviting me to audition for the role of Joan of Arc at the Park Lane Hotel, London. What wild excitement, what dreams of fame spun before my eyes! My mother and father were of course more sanguine and insisted that my mother would accompany me.

When the day came I wore a tartan pinafore dress with a square neck and a white blouse. I had white ankle socks and lace-up shoes. I was sixteen but had not yet graduated to stockings and heels. When we got to Park Lane a queue of hungry actresses wound around the block. This didn't appear to faze my Mother as she and I joined it and waited for a couple of hours as it inched forward. Then I was inside a darkened hall with a small, lit wooden stage upon which stood a young man. I had been told to prepare a speech from Shaw's St Joan and a voice from the dark explained that the young man would give me the cue and then I should perform the speech. The cue came and I said all of the first four words of the speech "thank you" came the voice from the dark "could we have the next". It was all over, except not quite, as we came out of the hotel a man with a microphone came up to my mother and I. It was MacDonald Hobley from the TV news and he wanted to know how I felt. I don't remember my reply and I certainly didn't know how I felt since I was by now completely out of touch with myself. But I guess my mother handled things and whisked me back home thus ending my brush with Hollywood although I had not given up on the theatre.

I moved over onto the arts side of the school in order to take English Literature and Language, French Language and Literature and Geography at A level although I had no idea what I was going to do with any of them. We were the School's first sixth form so there were only about eighteen of us; divide that by the number of A level subjects available to us and I was never in a group bigger than six. I was also entering the sixth form at an exciting time, when the stifling conformities of the fifties were beginning to come to an end and the liberating sixties were about to take off. As early as 1956 the Hungarian Uprising had given me my first moment of political awareness perhaps because by then we had a television and it was easier to get world news reports than reading a newspaper. But it also made a big impression on me and was in many ways the first stirring of my feelings for political revolution. In the same year John Osborne produced Look Back in Anger and by accident I discovered Simone de Beauvoir. I was sitting in the school library with a bunch of friends when one of them pulled a book of the library shelf. It was called The Second Sex and we only noticed it because of the word sex which was not a word seen out in the open in those days. We giggled quite a bit about it and lost interest when we saw it had no pictures. But for some reason I took it home and read bits of it in the privacy of my bedroom. I was both amazed and thrilled, it felt like at last I had met someone who felt like me and that I was not alone in the world any more.

I had two English teachers, Mr Hardacre who took us for English Language and Mr Pine who took us for Literature. In 1954 Mr Hardacre had started the Fifty Four club which was an after school club where we met in the School library and debated the issues of the day. He also encouraged us to keep what he called 'a commonplace book' in which we should make a note of our thoughts and literary experiences. I already had the habit of writing things down in random notebooks but now they had a name and were legitimised. Mr Pine was our English literature teacher and he used to invite the six of us who were taking Eng. Lit. to his flat in Watford on a Saturday afternoon. He made tea and toast for us while we sat and passionately debated Milton's Paradise Lost. He also took us to see West Side Story when it first opened in the theatre in London. It was so exciting and we were allowed to go on the stage after the performance because Mr Pine knew someone involved in the production.

As well as producing the School plays, Mr Lee was also having a profound influence on all of us in his A level French class. He brought in Georges Brassens records which he played to us on a School record player while we soaked up the poetry of Jacques Prevert and discovered Sartre, Juliette Grecco and the Left Bank. I was made for the existential, born to it really and related so intensely to 'The Outsider' by Camus that I resented anyone else talking about it let alone reading it. As an adopted child I always felt that I stood on the brink, on the edge of the beginning. I had no past history to look back on or to determine what might be a possible future. It would all have to be made up by me and created from the now. So when Mr Lee announced that the next school play would be Jean Anouilh's Antigone and I was chosen to play the lead, I was ready for it. The pump was primed and I didn't just play Antigone, I was Antigone and all my existential self fused with my teenage passion and revolt. Mr Lee took me to the hairdressers to have my hair cut an inch all over like Jean Seberg who Preminger had finally found to play St Joan. My Father, of course was furious with me, as far as he was concerned a young girl should aspire to look like Doris Day or Petula Clarke and most definitely not like Marlon Brando. When out of School I started to wear black from head to toe with long strings of black beads and I refused to wear any make-up except for dark eye liner. Bob Dylan had not yet arrived but the times were definitely changing and I felt I was out there, on the edge where I had always belonged. Needless to say I was a huge success as Antigone and decided there and then that acting was to be the life for me. However I was far from ready to fly.

At the end of that extraordinary first year in the sixth form Mr Lee arranged for me to spend a month in France. I was to stay with Madame Bernard who had a small pensionne in Brive which at that time was just a small town south of Limoges on the road to Spain. Mr Lee had stayed there and arranged for me to go on an exchange as Madame Bernard wanted her daughter Claudine to spend some time in England. It was the first time I had ever been away on my own and I remember rattling my way across France for what seemed like hours on end in a very basic train carriage with seats that were hardly more than lightly upholstered wooden benches.

Madame Bernard was a widow and very busy running the pensionne which Claudine had to help with since it was the school summer holiday. Nobody seemed to take much notice of me and I was very lonely. In the mornings several local women used to come in and sit round the kitchen table to help prepare the vegetables for the guests. I topped and tailed beans with them as the conversation bounced back and forth but I was much too frightened to try and join in with my limited French.

Brive was still not much more than a small, dry, dusty town whose buildings still showed bullet holes from the war and the pensionne was a very bizarre place. There was a very explosive cook who regularly flew off the handle and stormed out flourishing a lethal looking carving knife. And there was a woman of completely indeterminate age who did the washing up, cleaning and the laundry. She was a bit simple and wore many layers of clothes. At one point her face swelled up on one side and I gathered she had toothache. There was much arguing in rapid fire French but she refused to see a dentist and instead shut herself in the outhouse where the laundry was always hung to dry. She did not come out for two days by which time she appeared to have recovered and nobody seemed to mind.

Claudine was very busy helping her mother and I was not allowed out on my own. The major event for me was first thing in the morning when Claudine and I had to go to the local bakers and collect the French loaves. They were wrapped in big white serviettes and the baker used to give us each a most delicious cream slice filled with vanilla custard. Another trip we made together was to Claudine's grandmother's house to pick the peaches which grew in her back yard. The grandmother had died some considerable time ago and the house left just as it was with even a used cup left on the draining board. It was very dark, dusty and spooky and we had to walk through it to get to the peach trees. Picking peaches fresh from the tree should have been wonderful but it wasn't. Apart from the fact that coming through the spooky house had already filled me with fear, the trees were old, crowded and full of insects including mosquitoes which bit me all over.

Whilst I was there Mr Lee visited on his way back from staying in Spain and arranged to take Claudine and I out for the evening. We were not allowed out in the evening without a chaperone but it was arranged for Claudine's married cousin to come with us as well. We sat on the stone balcony of a somewhat fallen, grand hotel overlooking the dusty square. There was music playing for some kind of local festival and Mr Lee bought us a drink. It came in a small glass and was bright green. I guess it was probably Chartreuse but at the time I only knew it tasted awful and I surreptitiously poured it into a potted cactus.

Before he left Mr Lee arranged for me to meet him for a couple of hours in Paris on my way home. I imagine he wanted to show me the sights but I was dreadfully travel sick on the train from Brive and even threw up in the train corridor. So he took me to a bench on the Isle de la Cite where I slept before getting the ferry train for home. I had spent most of my time in France reading books that Claudine left lying around as there was nothing else to do. By the time I left I seemed to have passed through some kind of language barrier and could at least read fairly fluently in French. I was in France for a month and was not only lonely but dreadfully homesick the whole time. To this day I am constantly impressed by people who can go off to foreign lands for gap years or later in life, for adventures. It is something I feel I should want to do but I cannot. I have travelled a little in Europe and North America, on holidays and family visits, but it fills me with anxiety and I am always relieved to get home.

After that summer Mr Lee didn't return to the school for my last year in the sixth form. But he used to visit my parents home occasionally as he also performed in the same amateur dramatics group as my Father. He used to sometimes take me up to London and I rode side saddle on his motor bike with my skirts flying and my feet freezing. He took me to Ken Colyer's jazz club off Leicester Square and he introduced me to spaghetti bolognaise which he cooked for me at his flat in Chalk Farm. What I didn't know until many years later was that he had asked my Father if he could marry me and my Father told him to wait until I was twenty one and ask me himself. He wrote me one or two letters addressing me as 'chere animale' but he never made his feelings known to me and he certainly never took advantage of me. In turn I wrote back to him as 'Dear Mr Lee' because I could never make him into anything other than my French teacher.

Back in the sixth form we had a new French teacher who once again took on the role of producing the annual school play. It was to be The Lady's Not for Burning and to my great dismay I was not allowed to be in it as I was doing my A levels. My one great success at school in terms of public recognition and feeling good about myself was acting. So I left school still clinging to some distant hope of being an actor but with no real idea as to how to go about it.

4

Looking for myself

Deciding that I wanted to be an actor, though at the time I would have been called an actress, was a radical choice for someone of my class and family background, but my wise parents didn't speak against the idea. I suspect they knew that to do so would only push me further into revolt for I was still Antigone in my heart and soul. My father did not oppose my choice but undermined it by keeping up a steady stream of warnings such as continually reminding me that '90% of actors were out of work 90% of the time' etc. But maybe he was right and saw something unformed and vulnerable in me just as Miss Roberts had done all those years ago. I was a fairly accomplished performer but, in retrospect I see that I loved theatrical performance not only because the applause reassured me but because it gave me a script that held me safe. It gave me an outline, a sense of self-definition that I lacked.

While I dithered, my wise mother kept an eye on the jobs page of the local newspaper and eventually pointed me in the direction of an advertisement for a trainee library assistant. The job was at the research laboratories of the GEC at Stanmore which was only a bus ride away. So I applied for the job and was called for an interview. The research being carried out was for the Ministry of Defence and fell under the Official Secrets Act so the laboratories were shielded by a thicket of trees on Stanmore Common. The GEC were working on the development of a British missile called Seaslug which the scientists and engineers joked was run on an elastic band! The admin offices were in a large, elegant old house including the Library which had an Adam's fireplace and large windows that looked out onto a sweep of lawns. Beyond this were the single storey laboratories which had been added to the site.

I started working there in 1958, the same year as I left school and it was a perfect job for me. It had the feel of being safe and contained and yet involved in secret and exciting work since I had to sign the Official Secrets Act and show a pass to get in to work each morning. The Company employed a Librarian along with three junior assistants of which I was one. We had to work four days a week on site and go to the North West Polytechnic in Kentish Town once a week to study for the Library Association's First Professional and then Registration exams. After four years we would then be eligible to become Chartered Librarians.

In the mornings we three assistants had to collect in and then circulate the many technical journals on loan to the senior scientists in the offices and in the laboratories. This was great fun as we were provided with trollies to carry the heavy bags of journals around the site and duffel coats for when it was cold in the winter. We got to know everyone and were invited to all the different laboratory's Christmas parties. In the afternoons we had various library duties and mine included filing the regular updates of Mullard Valve Data. This was a time however, when solid state physics became a practical reality and the transistor arrived to take over from the valve. The age of electronic engineering was about to fundamentally change the world. Apart from the ubiquitous transistor radios that supported the growing youth movement and explosion of pop music, the coming of the transistor caused a small earthquake in the world of librarianship. The schedules of the Universal Decimal Classification system which was used for organising technological and communication data had to be extensively rewritten by a standing committee in Geneva.

At the GEC the Librarian and we library assistants were taken on a visit to the Mullard factory in Redhill to see transistors being manufactured. We were shown round the laboratories where there were long rows of women sitting with their hands thrust into things that looked like the incubators for premature babies. They were repeatedly picking up a tiny sliver of germanium with a fine brush and placing it onto the core of the transistor. They did this all day and the man showing us round told us that women especially liked the job because they could think about their shopping and housework while doing it. Little did he know that the Women's Movement was just around the corner!

This was also a time when the Cold War was taking over from where World War Two had left off. Any companies involved in the defence industries were rich with government money and could afford to treat their workers well. The GEC supported various after work social groups such as photography, music and a drama group. So as well as learning to be a librarian I could carry on acting and believing that I might one day be an actor. In the afternoons I sat and filed valve data and in the evenings I sat for the photographic club and performed in the Drama Group.

There were many branches of the GEC throughout the country and most of them had a drama club. Once a year they held a drama festival of short plays at the Head Offices in Wembley. Our drama club was run by Colin, one of the senior scientists who also loved theatre. By coincidence he decided to put on a short extract from Anouilh's Antigone as our contribution to the festival. Of course I auditioned and got the part and of course, I won the GEC national silver cup for the best performance. Like all amateur dramatic societies there were parties after the curtain came down which led to romances and love affairs. Colin who had produced Antigone, courted me and took me to see Joan Littlewood's production of 'Oh What a Lovely War' at Stratford East Theatre Royal. It was a fantastic experience and opened my head up even further to the lure of the theatre. Unfortunately he took me in his car which was one of the newly arrived bubble cars. Not only was I terribly car sick on the way home but also I was already spoken for.

In those days the general rule seemed to be that you captured a boyfriend and 'went steady'. If that worked out you got engaged and started saving for a place to live once you were married. This is what my eldest sister did and the side of me that wanted to please my family by being a 'proper' person, looked to my eldest sister as a role model. Towards the end of my time at school I started going out with a boy called Vince. We were not really suited but he'd asked me out and he had a certain status in school. He was talented at sports and was captain of both the School's football and cricket team.

I 'went steady' with Vince for almost five years while he did a science degree part-time, in the evenings at Brunel University, and worked at the John Dickinson paper mill in the day-time. We used to meet for a coffee at the Cookery Nook cafe on the High Street every Saturday morning and then go to buy a book from the range of orange Penguin paperbacks available at our local bookshop. In our plans for the future we were determined that our married home would have the books which our parent's homes had lacked. So our choices were based on what we might have heard of rather than any in-depth knowledge. In this way I read my way through a vast range of literature from Dostoevsky and Tolstoy, to Kafka and Grahame Green. In the afternoon Vince played either football or cricket according to the season. I used to meet him in the Compasses pub in the evening after the match with his fellow sportsmen and their girlfriends. The boys sat and dissected the game whilst we girls sat with a gin and orange and smiled. We didn't seem to have much to say to each other, least ways I didn't have much to say to them and it was very boring.

On Sunday's Vince used to come to my parents' house to collect me to for tea at his home. His parents were from Sunderland and had lived through the terrible years of the economic depression. They had come South for his father to find work and lived in one of the 'prefabs' that had been put up in the years immediately after the war to solve some of the housing crisis. They could never forget the hard times they had known and always worried they would come back. So an air of gloom always seemed to hang over them.

Vince and I had to walk across the park to get to his home from mine and since it was Sunday we wore our best. Vince had a grey suit with the newly fashionable narrow trousers and a slim Jim tie. I wore a full skirted dress pulled in at the waist with a wide belt and many petticoats underneath which I had stiffened with sugared water. On my feet I wore my beloved T-strap stilettos which I had bought with my first wages. When we got to Vince's we had tea, read the Sunday People newspaper and listened to 'Sing Something Simple' on the radio. Again it was very boring but on the walk home we would divert to the golf course for a quick grope in a bunker. We would have another extended kissing session at my back door until my father called out 'Margaret it's time you came in'. So that was it for four very boring years but I was fond of Vince, I was sure he loved me and I really wanted to do the right thing. But as in my childhood, whenever I really tried to be a 'proper' person, that other person that lurked within was always there and demanding a life.

About three years into this relationship I was coming home from work one evening and feeling the boredom of my life. My journey home involved changing buses and walking a couple of hundred yards between bus stops. Times were changing on the High Street. The fifties were over and the sixties were getting ready to swing. As well as the Cookery Nook there was a new coffee bar called The Chef which had spindly legged chairs, a bamboo curtain and the sound of an espresso coffee machine mingling with music in the background. This was where the cool people hung out; the forerunners of the Mods; young men in pastel coloured Perry Como cardigans and sharp trousers but I had never been in there.

Further down the road was the Three K's which was more like the Cookery Nook, although it had installed an espresso coffee machine. This was where I braved to go, to escape the crushing boredom of my routines and have a coffee on my own. It was almost the first grown up, independent choice that I had ever made and my heart was pounding with a mixture of fear and excitement. I, a single girl, was breaking her journey home to go into a coffee bar on her own. And it wasn't just the breaking of the rules, but the luxury of spending money on a coffee for no reason other than the adventure of it.

The place was empty except for me and the staff looked like they wanted to go home. I got a coffee and sat at a table close to the door. Since I couldn't just sit there and stare into space I got out the book I was reading and opened it up on the table before me. I was too excited to be able to actually read but I kept my head lowered to the page as I sipped my coffee. So I didn't see the man who came in until he came and sat opposite me and asked me to pass the sugar. I was very embarrassed but looked up at him as I pushed the sugar over. He smiled and almost before I knew it I found myself talking to him. He spoke with an accent and told me he was Russian. My heart raced. A Russian here in my home town! Yuri Gagarin had just been launched into space and now here was a Russian sitting before me! He told me that he had fallen in love with an English girl that he met in Russia but now she had left him for someone else. I listened, enthralled and since I had only recently finished reading Anna Karenina, I saw the pain of lost love etched on his face. When we finished our coffee it seemed quite natural to leave the coffee bar with him and let him walk me to the bus stop. Before we parted he took my hand, placed a kiss on it and asked if we might meet again. How could I resist! So I agreed to see him again after work the following day.

Now, I would like to say that I was naive and innocent in all this and I certainly was in terms of my life experience. However, when I told my parents the next day that I was going to see one of my girl friends for the evening after work, I added that I might stay over night. So my innocence must have been supported by a certain knowingness or maybe I had just read too many Russian novels! I met him after work the next day in the same coffee bar. We sat and stirred foam into our coffee and I told him how good his English was. He told me he learnt it from his favourite book which was 'Forever Amber'. I had never heard of this book but it didn't matter. Here I was in a coffee bar with a Russian, talking about books and it was wonderful. I felt like Simone de Beauvoir sitting with Jean Paul on the Left Bank. So when he invited me back to his place of course I went. I felt like an 'intellectual' and wanted to stay up all night smoking cigarettes, drinking wine and talking about ideas.

When we got to his bed-sitter a degree of reality hit me and I felt a tremor of nervousness. There was a gas fire, a single bed and bare lino on the floor. He asked me to put a shilling in the meter and turn on the gas fire whilst he went to somewhere at the back of the house to get us a drink. More reality crept into my bones. I knew nothing about meters and gas fires. I lived in my parents' house that was always just warm. I had no idea where the heat came from nor how you paid for it. I sat on the floor in front of the cold fire until he came back with two cups of tea. He invited me to sit on the bed since there was no other furniture and of course I ended up in bed with him although I am not quite sure how that happened. All I can remember is his body thrusting into mine while I stared over his shoulder into the darkness. No words were said and I just waited until he fell asleep. I lay for a long time, crushed between him and the wall until the dawn began to lighten the room.

Since I was still in my clothes except for my knickers I noted where the door was then slowly slid down the bed and off the end of it. I picked up my bag and my knickers and was out of the door as quietly and quickly as I could go. I was on some kind of automatic pilot that just instinctively knew what to do. I walked and walked as the day opened up until I came to the bus station where there was an all night cafe presumably for use by the bus conductors. I got myself a cup of tea and stirred in some sugar. My consciousness was beginning to come back and control was creeping in as I noticed that the communal sugar spoon was fastened to the table by a chain. I had to be at work for 8.30 a.m. so I left the cafe and found the public toilets. I put on my knickers which were still in my pocket, washed my face, smoothed my hair and caught my usual bus for work.

When I got there it was such a relief to be a library assistant again. In the afternoon I sat and filed my valve data. As I slipped the crisp white sheets into their dark blue folders it was so good to have nothing to think about except alphabetical order. It calmed me enough to be able to bring the experience of the previous night to the surface. At first my mind whirled but gradually I marvelled that I had survived and that no one else knew what I had done. I looked and listened to my fellow chattering library assistants and I felt a distance open up around me. A distance that translated itself into some kind of strength and a growing up. I never saw the Russian again but I found I now had the courage to do something about my relationship with Vince.

The following Saturday I met him as usual in the Cookery Nook and over coffee and scones I told him how bored I was and that perhaps we ought to finish things. Poor Vince said nothing and we walked the mile back to my house in silence. When we got to my front gate he finally spoke and asked if he should come in and get his records which were at my house because, unlike his parents we had a record player. That was all he said and I felt so mean and cruel that I couldn't go through with it. So we continued to 'go steady' and in much the same way. The only difference was that Vince suggested we had maybe waited too long and should get engaged.

A month or so later we both took a day off work to go up to London and get an engagement ring. We only lived twenty or so miles outside London but it was a sophisticated world away for us. I think that going there to look for a ring instead of to a local jewellers was, like the books we bought each Saturday, a part of our shared ambition to be something more than our upbringing. I remember it rained for most of the day and we wandered around the West End not really knowing what to do or where to go. We went into the Burlington Arcade to get out of the rain and here we found a jewellers and a ring. It was Georgian and set with garnets and seed pearls but it was too big for me and we had to leave it behind to be made smaller.

For two weeks I waited for the ring to arrive and increasingly I dreaded it's coming. When I finally had the courage to confess this feeling to my wise mother she told me that if I felt that way then I must not do it. So I didn't and when the ring arrived I broke off our relationship for good. I tried to give the ring to Vince but, ever the gentleman, he insisted I keep it which I did but I have never worn it and eventually gave it to my granddaughter.

I now felt sufficiently grown up and sure of myself to look for a change of jobs. My first move was to another electronics firm in Neasden called G & E Bradley who were a part of the Lucas Group and were working on the industrial use of the newly discovered science of the laser. The job of librarian involved obtaining and filing vast quantities of trade literature. The library was not really a library as such, just a small office built on top of the flat roof of the workshops. It was big enough to hold a desk for me and a bank of old grey filing cabinets for the trade literature. I hated this job, I was lonely and everything about it felt ugly but to get to my office I had to walk through the drawing office. This was a large airy space filled with handsome young men in sharp suits sitting with sharp pencils at their huge drawing boards. In this way I met and had a brief romance with Roy who had an open topped MG sports car and used to take me ballroom dancing at Richmond. It felt very romantic but unfortunately Roy was more or less committed to the daughter of a family friend and when it came to the moment he chose her.

I had one year of studying left in order to complete my Registration Exams for the Library Association but I badly wanted another job. This time I moved further into London and got a job at Hawker Siddely Dynamics whose offices were in Charterhouse Square in the Barbican. I was moving back into the world of research as they were working on Blue Streak. This had originally been a British missile but the Cold War was morphing into the race to conquer space. So when it failed as a missile it became the first stage of the European Space Launcher. The research was still all very classified however and my job as a librarian was to maintain the research files. I had a small room lined with triple locked cabinets that I had to unlock and lock either end of everyday. I had a huge bunch of keys with which to do this and it took ages before it was done and I signed in the keys to the Admin Office at the end of the day. Once again it felt more like a filing clerk's job and I didn't stay there for long. But it had moved my horizons into Central London and by the time I left Hawker Siddley I was a chartered librarian. I could now not only aim a little higher but had more choices. It was not long before I found myself a job as Library Assistant at the British Film Institute in Dean Street, Soho which also moved me over into the 'arts' where I felt more at home.

There was much that I loved about being a librarian. At college I was one of the few that loved learning and applying the classification schedules. This was long before digital access to information. The organization of knowledge was still hierarchical; its expression linear and its access through indexes was alphabetical. There was both a philosophical and political content to classification which had a big appeal for me. I also very much liked helping people and through their requests being continually exposed to new knowledge and ideas so the job was never boring. I think I also liked the fact that most of the libraries I worked in were within institutions which made me feel secure and a part of something greater than myself.

In the early sixties, just before I started work at the British Film Institute, the business where my Father worked collapsed and my father was made redundant. Never a man to give up he reinvented himself as a grocer, sold up the family home and bought a shop in Saltdean. He and my mother went to live in the flat above it and I remember my Father declaiming as we drove away from our family home "No one looks back!" My older sister was married by now and had her own home and my youngest sister and I were both committed to staying in London as I was working there and she was at college studying to be a speech therapist. So the two of us eventually found a place where we could share living together.

We had two rooms, one for each of us at the top of a small terrace house at Tuffnell Park. There was a sink, a cupboard and a stove on the small landing that served as a kitchen and the landlady lived in the basement with her dog. When we wanted a bath we had to ask her and she ran it for us in her bathroom. We were allowed two baths a week but we dreaded having them as it involved having to sit and talk to the landlady while the bath ran. She was obviously lonely and had told the neighbours we were her nieces because she didn't want them to know she was letting out rooms.

Moving home disturbed me and shook me up. However much I might have felt apart from my family home I also badly needed it to hold me steady. I have always said that it was my parents who left home not me. Without a settled centre I had no idea where the perimeter was and no idea of where to go for confirmation of who I was. So contrary to my Father's orders, I decided to look back in a serious way and go in search of my origins

As a child, my parent's bedroom had been a kind of inner sanctum which I used to sneak into whenever they were out. The great attraction was my mother's dressing table where she kept her jewellery box and a beautiful smokey blue, glass powder bowl. I loved to take the lid off and stroke the soft powder puff that sat within it. The dressing table was hung with triple mirrors and I especially liked to look at myself from the many angles it provided, wondering which one was the real me. My mother had a royal blue, full skirted chiffon dress for special occasions. It hung in her wardrobe where I liked to squeeze in and drape the chiffon around my shoulders, pretending I was a princess. It was on one of these occasions that I discovered the large tin box which my father kept at the back of the wardrobe.

One afternoon when the rest of the family were out I dragged out this box and rifled through it. It was full of official documents; the deeds of the house, birth certificates, medical cards and at the very bottom lay two pale green envelopes with sloping handwriting in black ink. I took out one letter and read it. I can only remember it was something to the effect that since Margaret Ann W no longer existed then the ten pounds that had been put into the Post Office account rightly belonged to the W family so could my father return it. The second letter conceded defeat and agreed that the money should be kept for me. Along with the letters was a buff coloured Post Office savings book which recorded a payment of ten pounds made early in 1940. The book was made out to Margaret Ann W c/o and a name and address in Helmsley. This was crossed out in official red ink and my name over-written with my new, adopted surname. I didn't take a lot of notice of it but I read the green letters over and over again. I noted the address at the top of one of them and then I put them back exactly where they were in the box along with the Post Office Book and carefully put the box back. Many years later when my parents were packing up to move house to the shop at Saltdean they gave me the Post Office savings book. They told me that my original grandmother had put the money there for me and that they'd had to fight to keep it for me. But they did not give me nor mention the green letters and of course I could not ask for them. I have always slightly resented this as those letters seemed to be such a vital part of the very small amount of actual physical evidence of my past.

However, although I had not written down the address at the top of those green letters I had also never forgotten it. So when I started my search I knew not only the names of my genetic parents, I also had an address. Was it at all possible the they still lived there twenty years on? I went to the Public Library and looked in the appropriate telephone book and to my surprise there they were, still at that address. I was thrilled to see their name in print, it made them real, too real really and I hadn't the courage to phone them so I wrote to them instead. My letter was apologetic and explained that I didn't want to make trouble; that all I wanted was to find out a bit about myself. I finished by saying that if it was too painful for them they didn't even have to answer my letter and I would understand.

It is only when I come to write the details of all this that I realise how strange it is. Some parts I remember with startling clarity, even tiny details like where the phone book was on the Library shelves. Other parts are so totally missing that I doubt my memory. Did it all happen or did I imagine it? I remember writing that letter but I don't remember getting a reply neither did I record any of this in my notebooks in which I have always written events and feelings. It was my genetic mother Mildred who recorded it and, fifty years later provided me with proof:

The letter on the doormat looked perfectly ordinary and innocuous as letters usually do. There it lay just waiting to be picked up. It was amongst others which looked like the electricity bill etc. so before I bothered to open them I put the shopping away and made a cup of tea.

What a shock! the letter was from Margaret Ann. She was living her own life in London and had decided to try and find us. She told us her address and begged me to go and meet her at an appointed time. I was stunned and rushed out to a phone box to phone Hal. He was as always, calm and sensible. He told me to stop crying as it was something to be happy about and he would be home as soon as possible. I felt quite deflated; I didn't want him to be sensible and calm. I wanted him to be in the same emotional state that I was.

Part of me didn't want to go and see her because I didn't know if I could cope with all the old hurts which I thought I had successfully managed to expunge from my mind all these years once again having to surface and be lived with again. Hal could not understand this, he thought I should be over the moon and happy. I didn't know what I was but I could not but agree to the meeting. It was Hal who decided.

What I do know for sure is that I invited them to tea on a weekend when my sister was away because all of this was an absolute secret from my family. It felt so dangerous and threatening that I couldn't share it with anyone let alone the people I loved and was terrified of hurting.

I walked down the hill to meet these errant parents at Tuffnell Park underground station and as I walked I felt sick with anxiety. What if it was true that blood is thicker than water. What if I saw them and loved them because of the blood! What if they hugged me! Even as I thought about falling into their arms in some all embracing love, I fled from any such imagined embrace. My parents, my parents! My lovely, loving mother! My Father who loved me and fought for me! How could I betray them. Surely blood could not overcome all that.

I cannot remember the details of the moment of meeting. Maybe I had just moved too far outside of myself, so that it all happened without my knowing. I remember being alone on the pavement outside the tube station and waiting. And the next thing I know is that these two people, these genetic parents of mine, are sitting in my flat, eating the tea that I have made for them. It is all as unreal as the salmon sandwiches, tea in proper tea cups with saucers and poured from a teapot, that I served up for them. Once again it is Mildred who provides the evidence:

> *The bedsitter was clean and tidy. On a table there were paints and what were obviously hand-made and painted Xmas cards in the making. So obviously she had inherited my artistic streak. She was quite small and thin with an educated voice. It must have been as difficult and emotional for her as it was for us. I had thought that I would immediately feel the bond between us and would want to gather her into my arms. But somehow I felt very inhibited, the years between had been too long. I had had no part in her growing up, formative years. There was a gulf between us that neither of us could cross at that moment. I prayed that it would right itself as I very much wanted to be at least a friend. But it was not to be.*

It was my genetic father Hal who did most of the talking at that first meeting. He seemed to just explain over and over again how they had no choice; it was a time of uncertainty; the war was beginning; they were young and had nowhere to live; All of which I now know to be true but at the time none of it felt to be about me and all of it about them. I felt their pain and I was upset by it. It all felt like my fault and here I was putting them through it all over again. I poured the tea, urged them to another sandwich and assured them that it didn't matter. I was alright, I'd had a happy life and they didn't need to worry about what they had done. I tried to set them at their ease like a hostess making my guests comfortable. After all I had invited them, I had started all this.

Then my father told me about their daughter. Some ten years after I was born they had another child who was grown up now and training to be a nurse. They loved her very much and she knew nothing about me. They had never told her about that first, terrible mistake. It was at this point that my mother spoke to me. She told me she was afraid that if they told their daughter about me she would turn against them. She told me she had already lost one daughter and could not run the risk of losing another. Her eyes filled up with tears as she told me all this and I felt even worse about making them unhappy. She begged me not to ever get in touch with this other daughter, my genetic sister, and of course I promised not to.

When they left we agreed to stay in touch though there had been no actual touching at this meeting. I walked them to the tube station and we said good-bye. We did not even shake hands, just a small wave as they disappeared underground. Then I walked and walked, nowhere dramatic, just around the streets until it was dark and the day had safely gone. I had to hold on to my external shape as the only thing I could count on to exist. As I walked I felt my feet making contact with the pavement and from my feet upwards I slowly dared to test the existence of myself. I stretched my fingers; felt my arms move against my body; brushed my hair back from my forehead. Yes, I was still there, but inside me there was nothing, just a big black hole that I dare not enter.

And there was another person, their other daughter, involved in all this. I had promised never to contact her but I found it hard to handle the knowledge of her. I was not hurt by her existence but by the fact that my parents had hidden my existence from her. Not only that but they had put the burden of their secret on me as well. This 'sister' stayed on my mind for many years and became a kind of focus for many of my doubts about the worthiness of myself.

I think it is true to say that there was one more meeting around this time but I cannot be sure. I remember that a letter came explaining that their daughter was going away for a weekend so would I like to visit them. I seem to remember sitting in their front room and them telling me all about their life together. They were walkers and showed me lots and lots of photographs of the two of them in the countryside. And that is all that I remember except that I felt incredibly claustrophobic and suffocated. But I cannot be sure if any of this second meeting is true or if it is a false memory. I did not keep their letter and apart from remembering walking down their street and looking for the house number, I can remember nothing of the journey.

What a dismal swamp of bad feelings swirled around these first meetings and none of it helped with my search for identity. In fact it only made things worse. I felt like a bad person whose very existence had only had brought pain and anguish and had to be kept hidden in case it brought further distress. I couldn't handle any of it and I left it alone for many many more years.

5

The Acting Lark

The dark side of me, the side of me that felt the only legitimate past that I had was that of bringing pain and unhappiness to people, was always at war with the part of me that was a loved and well brought up girl but who always felt slightly illegitimate in the role. So I became a performer who tried to adapt to whatever seemed to be required of me at the moment and over which I felt I had some control.

When I started work at the BFI there were already two other Margaret's working in the Library and Information Department so they asked me if I would mind being called Ann which was my middle name. This was not a problem for me given my tenuous hold on my identity. I was also so overwhelmed by all these clever, intellectual people that I just went along with it and became Ann at work for several years. However it certainly did add to my constant feeling of not quite being a real person and having to make it up all the time.

My parents had tried to bring me up according to their values forged in the conformity of the fifties. But I was now living independently and working not just in London but in Soho, as the sixties were starting to swing. It was a very creative time and never more so than in the world of film. The London Film Festival was established at the National Film Theatre on the South Bank which gave everyone a chance to see films from Poland, France, Italy and Japan. My sister and I went to one of the Festival's all night film shows. We sat through four films from ten o'clock in the evening through to something like five in the morning. The films we saw included Polanski's first film 'A knife in the water' which we both agreed, when we emerged bleary eyed into the dawn on the banks of the Thames, was completely beyond our understanding.

The Library supported the needs of growing numbers of film academics and the burgeoning number of film studies courses. It had books and journals on every aspect of the film world and just working there was a huge source of education for me. One afternoon one of the film academics, Peter Harcourt, who worked at the Institute, came into the Library. He told the Librarian that he had tickets for the matinee performance of Andorra with Tom Courtenay in the leading role and asked if she could spare someone to go with him. I was chosen simply because I happened to be there and so off I went to the theatre for the afternoon.

I was terrified of this clever, educated man and afraid that I might have to make educated comments on the performance so I kept very quiet. To make matters worse it turned out that Peter knew Tom Courtenay and took me round to meet him in his dressing room. They talked whilst I grappled with my first glass of neat scotch and afterwards Peter took me to dinner. As a way of holding my head up, I tentatively told him of my own theatrical ambitions. Although I had left the company I was still involved with the GEC Drama Group, returning there to act and at that time, produce a version of Thomas Dekker's 'Shoemakers Apprentice'.

About a week later he came in to see me in the Library. He told me he was having a get-together with some of his friends on Sunday and would I like to come since some of the guests were professional working actors. So I went to Peter's little suburban house in Hendon which at least presented no threat as it was the kind of place I grew up in. But inside the house there were far more books and far more clever people than there had ever been in my childhood. It was a hot Sunday afternoon and most of the action was happening in the garden. Peter introduced me to various people including Joe Melia and Eleanor Bron but I can't remember actually talking to anyone. As evening fell we moved into the front room and Peter's wife Joan served us up with dishes of pasta which we ate in bowls on our laps. The room was full and I sat on the floor with my back against a carved, wooden bookcase. All my attention was focused on the reality of that contact, of my back against the carved wood whilst the theatre of bright conversation floated before me. Fortunately I had a non-speaking part.

As it got late and dark I knew I needed to leave if I was going to catch the last tube home but I didn't know how to interrupt the flow of conversation. When the guests started to leave Peter was all the time busy seeing them off and I didn't know how to get his attention. In this way I was alone when he returned from seeing off the last guest. He brought a rose in with him from the front garden and gave it to me saying it was the last rose of summer. I took it and thanked him, not knowing what else to do nor where to put it once it was mine. Joan was in the kitchen clearing the dishes and I had been too paralysed to even offer to help; mostly I just wanted to go home. However Peter and Joan both suggested that since it was so late I should stay over. They showed me to their little spare room and brought up a clean duvet for me.

So there I was, in the little bed in their spare room when my host, who I hardly knew, came in and slid under the covers with me. Since I didn't know what the rules were in this kind of society, I carried on doing what I had been doing all day which was to silently go along with whatever was happening. But it wasn't horrible and I did feel cared for. The next morning we all, Peter, Joan, their two children and myself had breakfast together. It was very jolly with lots of jokes and laughter. Their two children were quite young, probably about eight and six years old and over the coming weeks, months and years I became their babysitter, spending most of my weekends at the house in Hendon. Peter and Joan no longer slept together and had separate rooms and when I was there he became my lover in the little spare room although he was always back in his room by the morning.

But Peter was also genuinely interested in my proposed career in the theatre and told me about the Unity Theatre at Mornington Crescent. They were a semi-professional company with an illustrious socialist history and at this time they were auditioning for their next production. The play was a new play called The Licence and centred on the marriage preparations of a young Jewish couple. The girl had discovered that her parents had been married on a kibbutz in Israel and had never actually had a marriage licence. It was primarily a vehicle for a debate about the founding of the kibbutzim and the ideology that sustained them. My new found family encouraged me to go to the auditions and I got the part of the young girl although I have no idea how since I must have been the only non-Jewish member of the cast. But it was a step towards being a professional actor and I learned how to sustain a performance as we played three nights a week for an eight week run. This was the first time I had ever done anything other than three performances for family and friends. I must have done all right since I got a positive write-up in the local Camden newspaper along with my photograph.

Most of my acting experience so far had to do with my inner sense of myself; my need to be defined by a role and get applause for it. My experience at Unity Theatre was more controlled and professional and should have been a point from which I could move on and move further into the business of acting. But it wasn't, because my person and my passion had been diverted. I was rushing back to Hendon after rehearsing and performing because, although I didn't realise it, I was not only falling in love, but this couple, their children and the house at Hendon had become a kind of replacement for my childhood home. I always stayed for Sunday dinners and when Joan washed her hair I used to pin it up in rollers for her; as a family we all went rowing on the Serpentine or rambling in the local woods; and I played with the children. At night I slept in my little bed in the spare room and Peter would come and make love to me. It may sound bizarre but there was a comforting stability and familiarity in it all. I was used to being a not quite legitimate member of the family. It was a role I knew how to play.

Then it all changed. One New Year's Eve Peter and Joan went to a party with their friends and I, as usual babysat the kids. In the small hours of the morning I heard them come in and expected Peter to come to my room as usual. I had never known them sleep together until this one night when they returned home, merry from their party and I heard them go together to Joan's downstairs bedroom.

I lay there in the little bed, shocked at the pain of my feelings. I had never thought of Peter leaving his wife and the family for me but now I was wracked with jealousy plus a kind of horror at realising what I had become in this family. It was a moment of growing up and time for me to leave. I waited until everyone was asleep and then I quietly got up, dressed and sneaked out of the house. It was about three in the morning and I could have got a taxi but I wanted to walk back to the flat I shared with my sister. I needed to push myself to my limits in order to find myself again. It was the early hours of the New Year and the streets were still surprisingly full. There were hung-over partygoers returning home; a mum and dad with a rather sad looking daughter tagging along beside them; and the odd lone bloke that is always walking the streets of London no matter what the hour.

My love affair, for that is what I now realised it was, did not end there however. I just grew up a bit and I decided to find a place of my own. Peter remembers this as my being unwilling to carry on what was now an undeniable love affair, under the same roof as my sister. I remember it as a part of leaving Hendon and the family and taking charge of my own self. I found myself a flat which was an L shaped room at the top of a house in Islington close to the antiques market at Camden Passage. This was when Islington was just on the verge of becoming gentrified and filling up with actors and media people and my flat became a kind of love nest for another couple of years.

I also needed to put some distance between myself and the Film Institute where this lover of mine was a frequent visitor. As luck would have it a job came up at the Royal College of Art for a librarian and indexer. This was at the time when Sir Robin Darwin was rector and Christopher Cornford had responsibility for the Library within the Department of General Studies. I started there the year after David Hockney left and was still there when Biba opened their first shop in Church Street. I went there a few days after it had opened with one of my fellow library assistants and bought myself the shortest mini-dress you can imagine.

Working at the RCA was a lovely job. The library was in a long, high room with one wall entirely glazed from top to bottom, looking out onto an inner courtyard. It had several butterfly shaped book stacks down the centre of the room each containing books representing the artistic and cultural content of that century. Just shelving books in the morning was an education. I learnt which artists were working when which writers were writing etc. and gained an overall sense of the prevailing culture at any given moment in time. Every year the Fashion School students had to put on a cat walk show as part of the finals for their MA. All the great fashion reporters from magazines like Vogue and Harper's Bazaar would be there and we College workers also got invited to watch and attend the strawberries and cream garden party that took place afterwards in the courtyard. Although I loved this job I had not given up on the theatrical side of me and I decided to be more serious about acting by getting some training. I enrolled in an all day Saturday class entitled 'Movement for Actors, Acting for Dancers" at the City Literary Institute. The City Lit. as we always knew it, was just off Drury Lane and was a wonderful place, completely devoted to education rather than the business of acquiring qualifications and offered a huge range of courses both intellectual and practical. It was here that I met an actor called John-Dunhill who was apparently running mime classes in an old school building off the New North Road on the perimeter of Hackney. This was only twenty minutes walk from where I lived so I decided to join his classes.

John was an immensely good-looking, crazy Scotsman with buckets of charm who had lived in France and learnt mime from Marcel Marceau. He had done a deal with the local education authority whereby in return for giving drama classes he could have the use of a former domestic science building in the grounds of an old school. At the same time he was trying to set up his own theatre company which he called Group Theatre and was made up of a number of struggling, out-of-work actors. As a part of the deal with the education authority he had also been asked to put on a production at the Crown and Manor Boys Club which was also in Hackney. The chosen play was Harold Pinter's 'A Night Out' and was to be performed over two nights in a hall off the Holloway Road. Since the club had no girls John asked me to play the part of Albert's mother.

This may have been the early sixties, but the English class system still ruled at the Crown and Manor Boys Club and it was run on the lines of an English public school. There were gilded scrolls of honour in the entrance hall and the ethos of hard work and fair play ruled the day. Quite how they came to have diverged into the theatre I don't know but as a part of this trip into the dramatic arts a number of the boys were taken to see Lyndsay Anderson's film 'If'. I remember having a furious argument with the boys who were outraged by the film. They told me how they were invited to play football once a year at Eton and how well they were treated, even invited to tea. With unshakeable conviction they told me how we needed these people otherwise we would have no leaders for the Country!

Back at Group Theatre John was planning a production of 'Waiting for Godot' and I was given the job of stage manager and prompt for the production. It was magic for me and a great learning experience. The actors playing Estragon and Vladimir may have been out of work but they were very good and they knew the business. I loved watching the rehearsals and plotting every move into the script. Plus of course, my existential self flew to the meanings of Godot, whatever they were. Having earned my keep I was then given a part in John's next production. I was to play Maria, the female lead in Buchner's play Woyzzek which we put on for a two night's performance. I was working with real actors who knew their stuff and rehearsing with them was thrilling. I still love to see shows in rehearsal almost more than a performance. It is that combination of pinning down meaning and plotting moves to suit; where everything is still an open ended adventure, that I find very moving

It was sometime after Woyzzek that Peter and Joan decided to go back to Canada and try to make their marriage work and I was devastated. I spent a last candle lit night with Peter, both of us drunk on champagne, and then he was gone. John Dunn-Hill drew girls to him like moths to the candle and I was so sad and broken hearted that I turned to John, not as a lover but as a friend for comfort. Before I knew what had happened he, along with half his cast of out-of-work actors and various artistic people were camping in my flat. Amongst them was Christian who introduced me to the music of Nina Simone and bought me an LP of her singing which he made sure he took with him when he eventually disappeared. He was Algerian French, very alternative and insisted on taking me to see a light show. This was held in an up stairs room in a pub in Camden Town where flowing colours such as you would find in a lava lamp, were being projected onto a large screen to the sound of soft music played live by a girl with long hair and a silver flute. The air was thick with marijuana and there were lots of people dressed mostly in bell bottoms, cheesecloth and a wild assortment of velvet or lace. There was more to come as Christian urged me out of the room and down stairs to the toilets where he asssured me that I would see something beautiful. He took me into a cubicle and pointed to where, hanging from the cistern on a thread of cotton was a twist of silver and purple foil from a chocolate bar. "Isn't it marvellous" he gasped. I didn't understand the beauty of it let alone the meaning but maybe I was just too sad inside.

Meanwhile John was planning to take a production to the Fringe at the Edinburgh Festival and I arranged to take the whole of my holiday allowance for a month and be a part of it. We were to perform a play called 'The Shop on the High Street' which was a Czech play set during the war and about the German invasion. I had a small walk-on part plus was to be in charge of the props. We were a ragged crew of amateurs and out-of-work professional actors who kept themselves just a little aloof from the rest of us. We all left at five in the morning to drive to Edinburgh in a beat-up old van that took more than twelve hours to get there.

We were joined by another company with whom we were to share premises and whose play would run alongside ours in the same theatre. This was in St Mary's church hall which was part of a big Catholic youth club and where we all lived and performed for the duration of the Festival. The other company arrived before us and was a little more prestigious. Amongst them were a couple of old time, once successful actors now slightly past their best and a handsome, ambitious, young actor who kept himself close to them intent on learning all he could. They had already installed themselves in the billiard room which was next to the kitchen and enabled them to cook big fry-up breakfasts for themselves and their chosen guests. We were on tight rations which included a huge tin of custard powder that John had got cheap from someone and became the mainstay of our diet. At the back of the theatre space there was a small projection booth which the handsome young actor had put his mark on and he was the only person to have a room to himself. For the rest of us the men camped out in the games room and the women in the music room.

The first thing we had to do on arrival and between rehearsals was clean up and paint the theatre. We worked round the clock painting miles and miles of white paint. But to our joy, we discovered the public wash house in Edinburgh. It had huge white baths with fat taps and oceans of steaming hot water to wash away our tiredness and our grime. I was also sent out to find various props preferably by begging and borrowing. If I came back with nothing John screamed at me to go away and not come back until I'd found what was needed. I was terrified for most of the time and hardly remember the actual performance except that the cast usually outnumbered the audience.

Throughout the whole time I felt completely unhinged. I was glad to be doing it for the experience and to fill the loss of my love affair from my life. But I had absolutely no idea of who or what I was and I ached with loneliness. One night I was woken up by a member of the cast because I'd had a nightmare and was sleep walking across the room. I think the drama of it came as a bit of light relief and everyone made a big fuss of me. Even the handsome young actor came down from his projection booth and took command. He said I needed a bit of privacy and he would take care of me. He took me to his little room and tucked me into his bed. Then to my horror he tried to get in with me. I got up, left the building in tears and once again I walked and walked.

Somehow I can always put myself back together if I can go to some kind of extreme that places me on the outside of things and where I am totally alone. Being completely contained within myself I find a kind of strength that allows me to go back into life and perform as a person. As the dawn came up I found myself sitting on a hill side and looking down over Edinburgh which looked so beautiful with the rising sun gilding the grey tiled roofs. By the time I got home from my month on the Fringe the dark, chaotic side of me had almost swallowed me up but I also knew that an actor's life was not for me. Acting for me was too tied up with my need to find a personal identity and I couldn't move from there to being a professional actor. Being a Librarian had always kept me safely tethered to the ground so I threw myself into my life and work at the RCA and cleared the actors out of my flat.

6

Coming of Age

The RCA library was there to support the students not only in their artistic endeavors but in their dissertation that they had to write in order to complete their MA. This might be on any subject so, as well as having a wide ranging book stock, the Library subscribed to many journals. This was before the days of digital data bases and Internet access to information, so it was my job to scan the journals and create a card index of any article or illustration that might support the students in their artistic development or their dissertation. I spent my afternoons reading anything from Studio International, to Cahiers du Cinema to Scientific American. It got that I had heard of practically everything but new very little about anything. It was also around this time that the Library inherited a collection of historic pattern books from the Textile Institute. They were huge books filled with samples of printed cloth from early times to the modern day. It became my job to catalogue them and I spent a lot of time unnecessarily looking through them just to enjoy the glory of them. It was also my first introduction to textiles and surface pattern which would figure much later in my life although I didn't know it then. As librarians we got to know many of the students and I joined in the student life of the College on the weekends by going to their parties and discos which of course lead to the occasional 'sleepover'.

When I had started my love affair with Peter I knew that it was important to get some contraception but felt too guilty to ask my own doctor. I wanted to be anonymous so I found a doctor at random close to where I lived and made an appointment. The first thing I noticed on entering the waiting room was a poster stuck up on the cream tiled walls which showed Jesus welcoming children into his arms. I knew I had come to the wrong place but before I could leave the receptionist welcomed me with a warm display of Christian kindness. However my stumbling and embarrassed request to the doctor was met by a sad, 'more in sorrow than in shame' shaking of the head. He promised to pray for me and I left empty handed.

The times however, were on my side since two miraculous events had happened. The first was the coming of the pill. Arguments were raging over it as some people saw it as a call for unlicensed sex and moral degradation. But for many of us it was a blessed relief from the awful anxiety of the week before your period. An agony of days wondering if you were going to come on. The second wonderful thing to have happened was that a family planning clinic opened up in London and publicly declared its intention to treat unmarried women. It was the first of its kind and the female students I knew spoke of it with something approaching awe and reverence.

So off I went to the clinic which was just behind Tottenham Court Road. I was shown into a waiting room lined with a collection of old books which, as a librarian, immediately made me feel at home. There were half a dozen other women waiting there and we all sat with our hands clasped to cover our ring finger. I took down one of the books which I found to be an early manual on sex hygiene. At the page I had opened it suggested that making love in a vertical position would aid contraception. Perhaps as a relief to my anxiety, I started to smile and then to giggle. I passed the book to my neighbour who also giggled and passed the book on until we were all smiling or giggling although still not talking.

Then it was my turn to see the doctor who, to my surprise was a woman as I had never seen a female doctor before. She took my details and told me about my contraception options. I asked about the pill and she stressed that they preferred to prescribe it as a last option since there were health issues related to it. She then handed me over to a nurse who took me to another room to show me how to insert something called a diaphragm. The very word filled me with fear and the sight of it with dread. This was all in aid of my passionate and romantic love affair and here I was squatting on my heels while another woman spread grunge on this thing and showed me how to push it up myself. It was horrible. I left the clinic clutching a brown paper bag containing the ghastly thing and with instructions to just practice wearing it but not actually use it. I had to come back the next week and report on how I managed.

I didn't manage. I didn't even try to manage. The diaphragm never left its paper bag. Everyone was talking about the pill and I knew that was what I wanted. I went back to the Clinic the next week; no judgements were made and I was prescribed the pill. It had taken all my courage but I had done it. So how come four years later I was facing the prospect of being pregnant. Simple really, it was just the foolishness of my heart. When my lover left me I was heartbroken and my commitment to him was to stop taking the pill since I was convinced I could never love anyone else. I had forgotten the power and ease of a one-night-stand after a party, when you are feeling sad and lonely and longing for a little love and comfort.

There were no do-it-yourself pregnancy test kits in those days. I went to my own doctor and had to phone him the following morning to get the results. I used the phone box outside the College since I needed to feel completely alone and private to get up the courage to do what I had to do. I had two sixpences in my hand. The first was for a call to my doctor who confirmed that I was indeed pregnant. I agreed to an appointment with him that evening to talk about what I should do. But I didn't go because I already knew what I had to do. I had thought about it so much during the weeks waiting for my period.

I knew I could love a baby even though I didn't know how to provide for one. But I wasn't thinking in these terms. What I knew absolutely was that I couldn't give a baby any lasting, comforting, longed for sense of security. I didn't even know who I was and where I belonged. How could I take responsibility for the emotional security off another, as yet unformed human being. The way I felt it was, that to have a baby was to commit yourself unreservedly to it and I didn't feel I had a real or stable self to commit. If I had a baby I would be inflicting on it all the pain and insecurity of being alive that I felt for myself. I just didn't feel equipped to bring another human being, especially my own child who I could love so much, into consciousness. It seemed much fairer, given the person it would get for a mother, to leave the baby snuggled in the darkness of its un-being rather than bring it into the light of day. This may sound very fanciful and as if I am making an excuse but it was exactly how I felt at the time.

A phone number circulated amongst the girls and women at the College. It was the number of a doctor from whom it was said you could get an abortion which at that time was still illegal. Such a number was like gold dust in those days. No one wrote it down but we all carried it in our heads and passed it around. The instructions that came with the number were that when the receptionist answered the phone you just had to say that you wanted to book a holiday. So I used my second sixpence, made the call and asked to book a holiday. The receptionist presumably knew exactly what it was about and I was told to come along to an address in Hampstead that Friday at 6pm. So I had done it, but on the bus on the way home from work I deliberately let go of all my reasons. I folded my arms across my stomach and let my emotions have their way. I thought about my darling little baby curled up inside me and I felt such a surge of love for it. Then in my head I kissed it and let it go. Great debates have always taken place about abortions and they continue to do so even though it is now legal. But when it was illegal I had friends who almost died from back street abortions and one who became sterile because they cauterised her in the process. I was lucky but I am quite sure that no woman undergoes an abortion or termination as it is now more discreetly called, without a great deal of emotional pain and trauma.

I made my way to Hampstead on the Friday as instructed and as I came out of the underground station found it had started to snow. Not soft flakes but wet, and driven by a cold wind that stung my face. It settled in a thin slush making it difficult to walk quickly and I could hear the church clock chiming six. I searched for the house number, scared that they would refuse to see me if I was a late. A woman opened the door of a large house and let me into a wide hallway. It had a parquet floor with a beautiful rug running along its length. There was a dark, tapestry covered bench along one side of the wall where I was told to sit and wait. I felt so embarrassed by the puddles of melting snow that gathered round my boots onto the polished wooden floor. Then I was shown into a surgery somewhere at the side of the house.

The doctor was middle aged with greying hair. He did not ask my name but was not unkind. He just asked me to take off my tights and knickers and lie on the examining bench. He examined me gently but without a word and then told me to get dressed. He said that my holiday would cost me three hundred and fifty pounds. I agreed to this and to meet him at an address in Harley Street at the beginning of the next week, with the money in cash and where he would be waiting in his car outside. I thanked him and left. I never knew his name and at no time was the word pregnant or anything medical mentioned.

When I was a child my parents opened up a small insurance policy for me, as with both my sisters and gave it to me when I left home. Because I wanted to be a good girl and please my parents, I had continued to pay into it. It was now worth just under four hundred pounds and so enough to pay for my abortion. As instructed, I met the doctor in his car in Harley Street and paid him the cash. He told me that in order to stay just within the law I would have to see a psychiatrist who would make a note of my unstable mental health. This was in case it was ever discovered and the only acceptable grounds for abortion in those days were if the mother's mental health could be seen to be at risk. He pointed out the house where they were expecting me then I got out of the car and never saw him again.

The house was a tall, narrow London house and I was shown into a room where an old man sat at a desk. He told me to sit down close beside him because he was a bit deaf. He asked me a few rudimentary questions about how upset and disturbed I was feeling. He hinted that I might even be thinking of taking my own life. But he didn't listen to anything I said in reply instead he wrote some answers to his questions using a blue fountain pen which I used to counter sign. The interview took no more than ten minutes. Then he told me to go downstairs where I would meet the surgeon who was also a woman. She told me to take off my lower clothes because she needed to examine me and shift my womb slightly to make the operation easier. After this she gave me an envelope which contained the address of the nursing home where the operation would be carried out. I was to go there the following Monday morning having had nothing to eat or drink and be prepared to stay over night.

It was all going like clockwork. I was part of a very well planned and well organised series of events. Apart from a dull ache in the small of my back I had no feelings at all. But for the first time in my life I went into a pub on my own and ordered a drink. The pub was dark and cool and had only just opened up for the evening so it smelt of polish. I sat and drank my whisky which I didn't like very much but I needed something harsh and external to focus my feelings. I took out the envelope and opened it. There was just a card inside with a number typed in the corner and the address of the nursing home which to my horror was in Hendon and only a couple of streets away from where I had lived in my ménage a trois.

When I first found out I was pregnant I told the guy with whom I'd had my one-night-stand and he was surprisingly kind and supportive. He said he would go along with whatever I wanted and even offered to help me pay for it but I refused. I couldn't involve anyone else in this terrible thing that I was doing; it had to be my responsibility alone. When I arrived at the nursing home they were very kind and gentle. They helped me into a pretty gown, gave me a pre-med and the next thing I knew it was all over. I had to stay the night and was given a light meal plus a big cup of hot chocolate to go to bed on. In the morning there was grapefruit for breakfast then I quietly packed my bag and left.

For the next two days I continued to bleed quite heavily and I became more and more frightened. It was the week before Christmas and I was supposed to be going to my parents' but on the third day the blood seemed to be coming away in lumps. I was truly frightened so I rang the Hampstead doctor whose number I still had. He told me not to worry but to go to my nearest chemist and ask them to phone him. He would prescribe something for the bleeding over the phone.

The chemist on Islington High Street did as I asked and after talking to the doctor on the phone gave me half a dozen small pills which he said would stop the bleeding. He then said that since this was all taking place within private practice he would have to charge me the full price for the pills which would be £10. This was the last straw for me and I dissolved into tears since all the money I had was for my train fare home and this was before the days of cash points. The chemist was really kind, took me into the back office and had his assistant make me a cup of tea. Then he told me not to worry and that I could pay for the pills later by opening an account which is what I did.

All that remained now was for me to get home and face my parents. To keep myself going I bought train tickets on the Pullman Brighton Belle which still had its velvet seats and little lamps with pink lampshades. I bought myself a copy of Vogue which I had never bought before but helped me suspend reality for the journey home. I knew I couldn't possibly tell my parents what had happened. My father had such strong moral principals and my mother, who loved babies had devoted both her personal and professional life to caring for them and protecting them. What I hadn't realised was that this loving and caring didn't just stop once you left home. The minute I walked in the house my Mother thought I looked ill and asked me what was wrong. I broke down in tears and confessed, all which must have shocked her deeply but all she said was "Well, we'll tell Daddy that you have flu. Now go to bed and let me look after you. We'll talk about it later" which we never did and my father never knew.

But I did write and tell my former lover about it since we had continued to write to each other even though he and his family were now making a go of it back in Canada. In response he suggested that I go out to see him and the family for a short holiday so I got myself an evening job in a pub to get the fare together. I flew first to New York because he was going to be there for a few days and he thought I would like to see New York. We didn't meet as lovers; I was certainly too emotionally wounded by the abortion to be able to even think about sex. But I also think that we both wanted, or maybe just needed, to put our relationship somewhere else since we didn't seem to be able to end it. Instead, we walked the streets of Greenwich Village and I thrilled at the idea of walking where Ginsburg, e.e.cummings and Ferlinghetti had also walked. We also spent almost a whole day in the cinema watching the seven hour long Russian film version of War and Peace whilst a woman sitting behind us loudly chomped her way through a bucket of pop corn and several packets of crisps. Then it was on to Kingston, Ontario via a one night stop over in Montreal so that I could experience French Canada. This was also the year of the Montreal Expo 67 when the radical community housing project Habitat 67 made such a stir in the world of architecture.

In Kingston I stayed with the family in their pretty little wooden house. I rode a bicycle along the lake front in the mornings and spent time with the children for we had missed each other. But I only remember having one day alone with my former lover. One hot, sticky day he took me for a drive to find a lake he knew of, somewhere near Battersea so that we could have a swim. As a Londoner this sounded promisingly familiar but the roads were dry and dusty and the houses few and far between. At one point the car over-heated and we stopped to get water from a ditch alongside the road. As he dipped in the water bottle, what seemed like a thousand frogs leapt, croaking into the air and some kind of snake slithered across the dusty road. I crouched terrified in the open-topped car. This was definitely not the Battersea I knew.

We found and swam naked in a lake where the water felt like silk which was wonderful although I couldn't stop worrying about what else might be there in those dark waters. Then as we sat eating our picnic an old guy came by and told us he had once caught a seven foot water snake where we had just been swimming. All my fears were confirmed and I began to realise that I was not quite up to this wilderness that is still so close to the heart of Canada. I was sad when it came time for me to leave but I clutched a Buffy St Marie album, a book of Leonard Cohen poems and I felt renewed and hopeful about my life. This was the year that Trudeau was campaigning for the presidency and as I walked through Departures the man at the barricades raised his two thumbs to me and called out 'Go! Go! Trudeau'

Ironically I came back from Canada restored by the knowledge that this man was still in my life as my father figure and friend, if not as my lover and we continued to write to each other for another forty or so years. On the occasional times that I visited my sister who now lives just outside Ottawa I would also call in to see him. He had finally separated from his marriage, had many love affairs and now lived alone. I saw him for the last time not long before he died. He was very frail and living in a posh retirement home full of rich old people waiting to die. We managed a crazy trip out for lunch with me pushing him in his wheelchair through Ottawa's city traffic where as far as I was concerned the cars were all on the wrong side of the road. Eventually we got down to a restaurant beside the river where we sat in the sunshine sharing a pizza and a bottle of wine and giggled over the adventure of our journey. Six months later and back in England I heard from a mutual friend that he'd been asked to let me know that my former lover, best friend and father figure had died. I got out the file of his letters to me and I didn't read them but I counted them. There were over a hundred and thirty of them which pleased me greatly. Then I crunched them up one by one and set fire to them whilst sitting on the floor in front of my wood burner. On what was a cold, dreary Autumn day they gave off such a comforting warmth and the soft, silver ash that they left behind seemed right.

Perhaps I was simply growing up but that first trip to Canada not only put my relationship into another place where it could continue in another way, it also did my self-esteem a world of good. It was the furthest I had ever travelled and there is something about confronting the wide horizons and big skies of North America that does wonders for one's self-confidence. I came back to England determined to take hold of my life and do something with it.

7

The Personal Becomes Political

My political self was also now beginning to take shape. Through the influence of my Mother I had a passionate belief in being fair. I have a distinct memory of my Mother cutting the last slice of peach in the tin into three so that I and my two sisters had exactly the same amount for pudding. Through my Father's life experience I learnt about the power of the English class system, although if you grow up in England it is almost impossible not to be aware of this. My Father was in many ways the epitome of Thatcher's self-made man and although proud of what he had achieved he was always aware of what it cost him. He told us how he started out in life sweeping up at a boarding school for the daughters of the rich. When this lead to a job as a chauffeur for a rich family and he came South to work for them the first thing he did was get rid of his Yorkshire accent so as not to be the butt of jokes. He successfully improved himself but always remained socially insecure beneath it all. He was very strict with the detail of our behaviour in order that we should not appear 'common'. We were taught exactly how to hold our knife and fork and we definitely never had tomato ketchup on the table. Later in life I learnt from my older sister that when we went shopping as a family he always insisted that we three children waited outside the department store because he felt it was 'common' to have had so many children. I suspect that this social insecurity was also the source of his furious arguments with me when I would not have my hair permed or dress as he felt was proper and correct.

As I progressed through life I definitely realised there was inequality everywhere and I also believed not so much in self improvement but that one had a duty to make a difference; to leave the world a little better than you had experienced it. And of course I was growing into the an era of change, revolution and protest. As a teenager I had discovered Simone de Beauvoir and the existentialists. My growing political sense pointed me towards Richard Hoggart and E.P. Thompson and I found my way to Virginia Wolf and Doris Lessing. My political education was well on the way but I had also not quite finished with the theatre.

I decided that if I couldn't handle an actor's life then perhaps I could teach drama and I applied to the Central School of Speech and Drama to do their teaching course. I was summoned for a whole day's audition which was a mixture of reading aloud, group improvisation and an individual interview. A week or so later I received a letter from them saying they couldn't offer me a place immediately since they had concerns about my voice and they had made an appointment for me to see their speech therapist. I immediately phoned my younger sister who was by now a professional speech therapist and asked her what was wrong with my voice. There was a long pause while she thought about it and then replied "well I don't know Margaret, I've never really listened to you"!

The Central School's therapist did however know. After listening to me she concluded that the crack in my voice was because I was pitching it below its natural level. She hinted that I was doing this deliberately for dramatic effect and that now it had become a habit. She said that with a year's therapy she could raise the pitch of my voice and so 'cure' it. I was outraged. How dare she suggest that I had been pretending all these years. As far as I knew I had just always spoken the way it came out. Then doubts began to set in. Maybe she was right. Perhaps my cracked voice was related to my feeling of not quite being real and having to perform in order to be. Whatever was the case, I could not cope with having my voice changed so I gave up on the Central School and decided I could do it alone.

I knew from John Dunn-Hill's experience that the local education officer for Hackney was very forward looking so I went to see him and asked him if there were any youth clubs or groups that might want some drama lessons which I would give for free since I wanted the experience. He arranged for me to meet the man who ran the Pitfield Youth Club at Shoreditch School, deep in the heart of Hoxton in Hackney which, unknown to me, was still a very deprived and very wild area. The leader of the Youth Club didn't think I could handle the boys and arranged that I should take a girls only drama class one evening a week.

He was right of course and the girls were difficult enough. I planned classes of movement and improvisation and the girls spent most of the hour collapsed in giggles. The only real success was the night I took in my box of stage make-up. They painted their faces in lurid colours and then ran screaming out into the street to frighten everyone. The boys meanwhile were not happy at being excluded. We worked in a classroom which had a door with a small window in it and opened onto a corridor. Throughout the hour's session boys would run past the door and bang on it or pull faces up against the window which reduced the girls to even more hysterical giggles.

In my liberal, middle-class, infinitely understanding way, I decided that the boys simply wanted to have some attention and be part of it all. So one evening I opened the door where two boys, Wally and George stood grinning and invited them in to join us. The girls huddled in a corner whilst the two boys strode in and looked nervously around. I pulled out a table and chair and told Wally to sit and pretend to be the boss of a factory. I told George to go out and then come back in to ask for a job. It felt like success as Wally sat down and George went out closing the door behind him. A minute went by and we all held our breath until the door burst open and George flung himself down in the chair opposite Wally. "I wonna job" he demanded to which Wally answered "well you can't have one so fuck off!" The girls of course fell about in paroxysms of giggles and I was well and truly 'fucked' as Wally would have said. It was the end of my acting days and I'd had enough drama to last me a lifetime.

But I still wanted to do something useful with my life other than being a librarian. I wanted to make a difference. At the same time as pointing me in the direction of the Pitfield Youth Centre the local education officer had also told me about an experimental youth project operating out of a cafe for disaffected youth, further down Pitfield Street. He gave me the phone number of the youth worker currently running the project and suggested I get in touch with him, which is what I now did. The voice on the other end of the phone was soft and American. He told me that his name was Glenn and we arranged to meet at the Cafe Project one evening a couple of days later.

When I got there I found the Cafe closed and the windows boarded up. While I waited for Glenn to turn up a few young lads smooched up and started hustling me. There was a lot of pushing and shoving and somehow or other I managed to trip up and fall. I was very frightened but so were they and in that pause I jumped up and ran for it. Glenn phoned me later to apologise for not being there and explained that 'the boys' had smashed up the Cafe which seemed to be a regular occurrence. While we talked he told me about a project he was taking part in the following Bank Holiday weekend down in Brighton. He invited me to join it and that is how I met Glenn.

It was a time when the Mods and Rockers were fighting and sleeping on the beaches of Brighton. I went with Glenn and a group of like minded people who had organised to collect up any stray young people and offer them a mattress to sleep on at the Quaker Meeting House, the aim being to keep them out of the hands of the police. So Glenn and I had been up all night when we started to talk politics as we sat together in a bus shelter on the Brighton front watching the sun come up and flood the surface of the sea with the dawn light.

We talked about the world and its inequalities and about what one could do about it. What I brought to this conversation was my passion about the inequalities of the English class system along with a kind of low level political consciousness that you grow up with in the marrow of your bones if you are a part of that system. Against this was Glenn's can-do American energy and his freedom from the restraints of English class. He was Afro-American and brought up in Washington Heights, a tough suburb of New York, traditionally full of crime and drugs and not unlike Hoxton. His experience of inequality had a source quite different to mine and he was politically informed by the growing Civil Rights movement in America.

On the train back to London we continued to talk, not about ourselves but how it might be possible to make a difference. We talked about the Hoxton Cafe Project where Glenn was working and both saw it as an example of English social work at that time. He described how the cafe project was set up by a group of well meaning established people who did not live in Hackney but wanted to do good. They raised the money and appointed two workers to run the cafe. He described how the Cafe was constantly under attack. The boys would physically smash it up and the workers would put it back together again; an endless repetition that had changed nothing other than wear out a succession of well meaning workers. My reaction to this was to rage against wealthy do gooders and middle class social workers who patronised the have-nots and at the same time ensured themselves a good wage by getting the working classes to lean on them.

This was a time when revolutionary events and theory were surging ahead in South America and amongst the Civil Rights Movement in America. We both agreed that change could only come from the ground up but we both wanted to intervene as a catalyst for change. We talked about how one could legitimately work in an area such as Hoxton and not be patronising. We agreed that at least the shop keepers were legitimate providers so maybe we should think about opening a shop. As the conversation went back and forth we grew increasingly excited with each other so that by the time we got to London we had not only fallen in love but more importantly we had the raw outlines of a project. As a librarian and from my own life experience I knew the power of books. Glenn was self educated and had not learnt to read until he was twelve but having discovered books they were the saving of him. We noted that Hackney had five comprehensive schools, many adult education colleges and not a bookshop in sight, so we decided to provide one.

Once back in Hoxton, Glenn did not attempt to resurrect the cafe project but allowed it to self destruct. I carried on working as a librarian and supported Glenn to allow him to get our project off the ground. We gathered together like-minded people some of whom were either from Hackney or had connections with the Hoxton Cafe Project including Nancy who was Glenn's co-worker at the cafe and also an American although from the other side of the coin. She came from a very rich, right-wing family and had studied French at one of America's top universities. She had then gone on to work in the theatre in France and ended up in Hoxton of all places, because she too wanted to make a difference. After her work at the Cafe she began teaching French at Shoreditch school and used her theatre experience to put on a pantomime of Puss in Boots with some of the young people in Hoxton. They performed it out of the back of a van and toured the street markets with it.

At first I was unsure about the idea of a bookshop, in part from my own early English class experience. Even though I was a librarian I knew the experience of entering a bookshop with all its challenging shelves of books that I had never heard of let alone read and I thought that, like myself, people mighty be put off. But as an American, Glenn knew of other kinds of bookshops where they were not hushed library like places but where you could drink coffee and listen to music while you thumbed through the books. So we decided that the bookshop would have a cafe as well. We named it Centerprise and it became one of the first bookshops in this country to have a cafe. Gradually the project gathered momentum and I began trawling through the Charities Yearbook, writing letters in an attempt to raise money.

After months of not really getting anywhere Glenn decided that we would only be taken seriously if we had an address and a telephone. Two or three of us put in some money and we rented a small room as an office above a shop in Matthias Road, Hackney. We also registered ourselves as a charity and gained the support of ILEA which at that time was London's inspired Education Authority. In keeping with mine and Glenn's initial rejection of making money from the hardships and needs of the people, we wanted the bookshop to be non-profit making. We decided that any money it made would be put back into Centerprise so that it could support other community projects. The fact that we hoped to contribute the income of the shop and cafe to the community played a large part in our success at raising funds. We were eventually offered a large grant from the Gulbenkian Foundation but it was conditional on our finding someone to stand as guarantor against our proposed annual income of the bookshop.

Just at this time an old friend of mine got in touch. Hilary had been one of the library assistants at the RCA and left because she wanted to hike the hippy trail to Nepal. She got in touch to tell me she had done it and was now back in London. We met for coffee and she told me all about her adventures; how she had been stoned in Afghanistan for wearing a short skirt and lost all her clothes when she put them out to dry on a roof where she was sleeping in India and they blew away. She finished by telling me she had met a millionaire who took her gambling and, in her words, wanted to do good in the world'. At first I didn't believe her until she opened her bag to pay for the coffee and I saw it was stuffed with notes. Here was my opportunity. I told her about Centerprise and she arranged for me to meet her millionaire.

They picked me up from home in a taxi and he took us first to Wheeler's Fish Restaurant in Soho where we began our evening with champagne cocktails and I told him about Centerprise. After we had eaten he took us on to a night club full of sleazy stockbroker types on the make for any available female. Then we went to the Blue Palm Casino somewhere near Berkley Square. He played the tables whilst Hilary and I drifted around and stole a hairbrush each from the lady's loo. When we came out at around 3 a.m. he gave us each a hundred pounds from his winnings at the tables before taking me home in the taxi which had continued to follow us around at his request. But he came up trumps and agreed to stand as guarantor for the bookshop income. This released the Gulbenkian Foundation grant and Centerprise was ready to go.

One of the consequences of straddling two worlds, the conventional versus the alternative; the legitimate versus the illegitimate; or the revolutionary versus the librarian, is that I have never quite succeeded in being or doing anything really well. So it was with my loving relationships. I seem to make a habit of choosing extraordinary, creative outsiders and then trying to pull them into the conformity of what is proper and normal. Glenn spoke to my political self and he was an adventurer. He had fled the US to escape the draft for the Viet Nam war, spent some time in Europe and then hitch-hiked the hippy trail to Nepal. On his way back he stopped on a kibbutz in Israel for almost two years and only left when the six day war started. He had the most amazing passport with a pull-out extension covered in exotic looking stamps and visas.

By the time we had set up Centerprise Glenn and I were living together. But when he moved in to my flat I told him that I did not want a love affair, I wanted a committed relationship and I wanted a baby. Having a baby was a very real need in me because more than anything I wanted to have that flesh and blood relationship that I had never had and Glenn was happy to go along with my need. In all our discussions about our future we never talked about marriage both of us seeing it as a somewhat bourgeois institution. This was a also a time of revolution for women and I subscribed to the prevailing ethos of the Women's Movement that you could have a family without giving up your identity as a working woman.

However, once I was pregnant my Father began phoning me regularly on the subject of marriage. I had already had the words 'nigger lover' hurled at me from the street and my father was worried that my baby would have problems enough with being mixed race, though in those days the word would have been 'half-caste'. He insisted that I should not make matters worse by, in his words 'thrusting illegitimacy upon my child'. So to please my parents Glenn and I got married because I wanted to do the proper thing by them, but as ever I did not do it properly.

I was seven months pregnant when we got married, one afternoon at Wood Green Registry Office. We told no one what we were doing except our close friend Nancy because she had a car and could drive us there and we both went to work in the morning. However just before we set off I felt really bad towards my parents and I phoned them. My mother answered and I told her I was just going off to get married. All she said was "Oh Margaret" but I heard her voice wobble with what sounded like tears.

As well as it being the era of revolution it was also a time of peace and love. I was never a real hippy and always a librarian who loved the precision of cataloging and classification. But I had my hair in two long plaits; I believed in peace and love; and at home I wore long cheese cloth frocks and skirts. I was married in a cotton mini dress that was embroidered all over with sun flowers and that I bought from a shop called 'Forbidden Fruit'. I did not change my surname and I did not have a ring. Instead, when it came to making our marriage vows Glenn gave me a necklace made of red and brown beans that he had brought back from Nepal. Nancy was our only witness so we had to get a passing person to be the second witness.

It was not until we stood before the Registrar that I think we both realised we were doing something a little more important than we had thought. Things felt very tense when we went to sign the marriage certificate. They asked Glenn for his father's occupation and when he told them his father was a longshoreman he had to explain it was the same as a docker. The woman taking down the details smiled up at us, presumably hoping to relieve the tension but only making it worse as she said "Oh is that what you call them in Jamaica" and Glenn replied through gritted teeth "New York actually". When we came out of the Registry Office everything started to come right, even if a little bourgeois, as Nancy had secretly told a number of our friends what was happening and they were all waiting there for us. She had packed a hamper with food and wine and we all went and had a picnic on Hampstead Heath. The next day, through the post we received a large greetings card with silver bells and flowers on it. It was from my Mother and Father and came with love and best wishes for our wedding day. I knew it was my Mother's work and I felt so guilty because I also knew she really did want me to be happy.

Glenn and I were both convinced that we could have a child without it making any difference to our lives although when I got pregnant we did move to a bigger flat at the top of Highgate Hill. It had three big rooms, an outside toilet and was very damp and very cold but it was cheap. The only heating we had was a couple of old paraffin stoves and a small gas fire in the back room. But it was always full of people as we gathered together to plot, plan and fund raise for the bookshop. I continued to work full time until two weeks before my baby was due but the RCA were really good to me and made sure that I had a lot of work that involved sitting down at a desk. They also gave me two months paid maternity leave which was pretty rare at that time. Stephen who was a young lad from Hoxton, came to live with us as he needed to get away from home and Glenn reckoned he could help us in the flat in return for his keep. The three of us used to play scrabble well into the night when I couldn't get to sleep.

My daughter was born just before we opened the bookshop on Dalston Lane. I was registered to have her at Charing Cross Hospital on the Strand and had an appointment there on the Monday. She was two weeks past her due date so they were going to induce my labour. I didn't want this so I went to a party with Glenn and the Hackney crowd on the Sunday evening and danced into the small hours. It must have worked because I woke at about 5 a.m. to the early stages of my labour. I woke up Glenn immediately and with a degree of controlled panic, he woke up Doug, an Australian friend who had stayed over from the party, and had a van which meant he could drive us to the hospital. The problem was that he had lost one of his contact lenses at the party when he had got very drunk and cried. This meant we first we had to find a chemist to buy him an eyepatch so he could see to drive.

I arrived at Charing Cross Hospital on The Strand in a beat up old van, accompanied by an unshaven Australian with a black eyepatch and a stunned looking black man with wild Afro hair. The hospital were not too sure which of these men was the father and I was too frightened to explain although it must have come clear because Glenn stayed with me as my labour went on through the day. However, I was a too tired to get the job done and at the end of a day in labour they put me out for a night's sleep. I was terrified when they woke me up in the morning and re-started everything with a drip in the back of my hand because I now knew of the pain to come. What I didn't know was that it was going to get even worse. With each increasing wave of contractions I felt as though my whole self was going to disintegrate. At one point I threw up all over Glenn who had stayed at the hospital through the night and whose hand I wouldn't let go.

And there she was, this beautiful little baby girl of mine. She had such translucent, pale coffee skin and thick dark hair. I know all parents find their baby beautiful but I knew mine was the loveliest in all the world and I felt so privileged. But I was also totally unsure of how to play the role of a new mother. In those days it was standard procedure to keep you in hospital for five days after giving birth. On the second day Glenn turned up with Stephen and brought me a lampshade frame and some raffia because he thought I might get bored and want something to do. So while the other mothers slept and looked beautiful in pastel shades, I sat cross legged on top of the bed and made a lampshade.

We named our daughter Shoshannah because Glenn reckoned he had found himself beneath the desert skies when he was living on the kibbutz. We went home from the hospital in Doug's van with Stephen fussing over me and Shoshannah dressed in the dearest little red riding coat and hood that my sister had knitted for her. When we got home Stephen had already made up bottles of feed for Shoshannah and wanted to show me how to hold a bottle properly. I knew that I was going back to work so although I had a couple of goes at breastfeeding I hated it and was glad to have the excuse to give it up.

I loved and wanted my daughter so badly and I wanted to do the right thing although I didn't know what that was. My parents came to visit soon after she was born but they lived a long way away. I lived and moved amongst people whose main concern was to make the world a different and better place so I felt very alone in my mothering and Shoshannah was only ten days old when she went to her first Centerprise meeting. Glenn of course loved her as much as I did and like all new parents we spent many times gazing at her and picking out the bits that looked like him and the bits that looked like me. It was during one of these times when she was seventeen days old that I suddenly also became aware of the new person that was there. The person that did not look like either of us and was a mystery to us both. It made me feel very responsible towards this precious new person that I had brought into the world.

Births and marriages are so intertwined with family and I was never quite sure where I began in relation to family. Although I had only sent them the occasional Christmas card in these intervening years, I did now write to Mildred and Hal to tell them about my marriage and new baby:

> *Margaret wrote to let us know that she had now married and had a beautiful new daughter. I wrote back to say all the usual things, hoped she and the baby would be happy and as we would love to see her could we arrange a meeting. We never heard from Margaret again. I was left with the feeling that she had not really considered our feelings very much. She just needed to find us for her own satisfaction. Maybe we deserved it?*

She does not mention it but I have a set of cutlery that they sent to me as a gift. I also have a very powerful memory that in the card that came with it they used the word granddaughter in relation to my new baby daughter and I was shocked. No she was not their grand daughter, she belonged to my parents; the family who had loved and nurtured me. I remember feeling strongly that I didn't want these original parents to know my daughter. That I needed to deny them that joy out of loyalty and as my gift to my mother and father. Maybe I needed to abandon them as they had abandoned me although reading Mildred's words now I feel very mean and guilty.

I fitted in mothering my baby between Centerprise meetings and going back to work two months after her birth. The RCA was a post graduate college so many of the students were older and had families. One of them who had a child persuaded the College to set up a child care facility initially in a spare room. As it gained in use the College converted one of the mews cottages that they owned into a proper nursery so I was able to take Shosh into work with me. I used to wrap her in a blanket and tuck her into a sling. We had to get a bus down the Archway Road to Essex Road where we could get the 73 bus to Kensington Gore. This was in the days when the engine was at the front of the bus and gave off a certain amount of heat. It was a long slow ride across Central London so I liked to try and get the front seat where it was warm and Shosh and I could cuddle up and go to sleep together. The fact that I had a nursery available at my workplace was fantastic and was what made it possible for me to go back to work so soon. Shoshannah was close enough for me to be able to go and see her during my morning and afternoon breaks and feed her during my lunch break. The College was closed to students during the summer break so I took Shoshannah into the Library with me and she learnt to walk holding on to the Library shelves.

By the time she was two years old Centerprise was a great success and becoming an integral part of the community. I was beginning to realise that I would eventually have to find a job with hours better suited to being a mother and I also wanted to be a little closer both geographically and in spirit to Centerprise. So I found myself a new job as a librarian at Hackney Downs School and moved Shoshannah to a new nursery The school was colloquially known as 'The Grocer's' as it was once a grammar school and filled with the sons of the Jewish community in Hackney. When I started work there it had fairly recently become one of the new comprehensive schools and catered for the growing West Indian community in Hackney. It did however still have a separate kosher dining hall and a good quarter of the library cards in my library loans system had the surname Cohen. It was also a good school because it also still had most of its old grammar school teaching staff many of whom had fought in the Second World War and still carried the 'Spirit of 45' within them. They believed in the power of education to make society a better place and they also helped to stabilise the school while it went through its transition.

I had been a part of the founding of Centerprise and at one point was even the treasurer. This meant that I had to buy the National Insurance stamps for the people working there which I found an awesome responsibility. But by the time the project was established and operating in the community I had no formal working role in it. However I did become a kind of channel of connection between the school population, both boys and staff, and Centerprise. One day the Special Needs teacher came to the Library and told me about one of her pupils named Vivien. He was a lively twelve year old who, at that time lived in a Local Authority children's home. The only way she could get him to be still was to tell him to sit down and write a poem which he promptly did. She handed me a crumpled sheaf of these poems to read because she thought they were wonderful and indeed they were quite extraordinary.

I took them home to show Glenn because one of the newly forming ideas at Centerprise was to publish local people's writing. I typed them up onto wax stencils which we ran off on the roneo duplicating machine upstairs at Centerprise. We stapled them into a booklet with a hand drawn cover and sold them in the bookshop for 5p. They were such a great success that we produced a second properly printed edition with a photo of Vivien on the cover. This little book of lovely poems eventually went onto the CSE exam reading list at the time and it launched the Centerprise Publishing Project. Glenn and I had both read and been very influenced by Paulo Freire's 'Pedagogy of the Oppressed'. We were both inspired by his belief that traditional literacy programmes were one of the means by which the oppressed absorbed the values of their oppressors. That one needed to lodge literacy programmes within the experience of the oppressed to enhance their control over their lives. But idealism can rarely transcend reality and years later Vivien very sadly died in a terrible fire at his girl friend's flat when he was still only a young man.

In keeping with our belief that we should not make a living out of helping anyone less well off than ourselves, Glenn and I had always said that we would only stay with Centerprise for three years. By then either the people would want it and claim it or it would come to a close. We talked about what we would do after that and we decided that we would go to Chile because in Allende it now had a democratically elected Marxist leader so I began to learn Spanish at night school in preparation. Of course Glenn and his fellow workers didn't just abandon Centerprise. They set up regular meetings with members of the community and the local Council who agreed to continue to support it so that it would be left in good hands as indeed it was. It evolved and changed as the community changed but it did not close down. It became an umbrella for many community projects and continued to operate as a bookshop and coffee shop for another forty years.

8

Things Fall Apart

C enterprise had always been at the centre of our relationship so perhaps it was inevitable that our leaving it would affect our life together. Not only that but Allende had been deposed by a US/CIA backed coup d'etat and had committed suicide so that was the end of our Chile dream. There was one more shock to come as well, when Glenn told me that he had met another woman whom he couldn't put aside. Foolishly I told him to go and stay with our friend Nancy while he sorted himself out and decided what he wanted. For six weeks or so he would come and see Shoshannah at her bedtime and then have a coffee with me. We would sit and talk politics as we had always done and then he would leave. Only at that point did I ever allow myself to cry. Eventually he moved in with his new woman in her tiny basement flat in Hampstead. For many weeks I didn't tell anyone in my family that Glenn had left me and when I finally did my Mother was quite tearful. I just remember her saying, "Oh Margaret, if only we hadn't made you get married you might still be together". This wasn't true of course but I always felt it was her way of telling me that she accepted and understood that my life had to be other than what they might have wished for me.

When I first started working at Hackney Downs School I had found a small private and not very professional nursery for my daughter. The young girl who looked after the room she was in was a big Elvis Presley fan so the main thing Shoshannah learnt whilst she was there was the words and music to his songs. It was also a complicated journey as I had to walk with her in the pushchair down to the Archway Road and get a bus to the nursery at Muswell Hill. Then I had to get another bus to Finsbury Park, take a short walk and another bus to Hackney and do all this again in reverse in the evening. It had always been difficult but now, as a single Mother and a lonely one at that, I needed to make things easier for myself. As ever I solved my life problems by getting another job. This time it was as a part-time cataloguer at the ILEA Media Resource Centre which was just one bus ride down the Holloway Road.

Once again I found myself on the cusp of change but this time regarding the organisation and dissemination of knowledge and information. At the Media Resource Centre I was cataloging not books but audio tapes, film strips, video tapes and all the new educational media that was becoming as prevalent as books and print on paper. The new media required a different set of cataloging rules for entries that would be generated not by typewriter onto paper but by computer into data bases. The British National Bibliography had just started to use and develop Machine Readable Cataloguing (MARC) and the language of PRECIS indexing was being formulated and refined. PRECIS indexing involved allocating codes to the words in any title according to the function of that word in the sentence. This allowed the computer to read the codes and organise them into appropriate index entries.

My boss at the Media Resource Centre was keen to move with the times and I was sent on a course run by the BNB to learn the mechanics of PRECIS indexing. We then used it to prepare the catalogue entries back at the Media Resource Centre. For a whole year I spent my afternoons at work allocating codes to words according to their function in the title of pieces of media. It was all very esoteric but I loved the precision and quiet thoughtfulness of the process. This was also a time of industrial unrest and the Three Day Week. As I pushed Shoshannah home in the pushchair I used to pray that the street lights would not go out indicating that there was a power cut. One of the first things I used to do when we got home was put on a Jackson Five album and the two of us, my daughter and I would dance like crazy to Rockin' Robin. A power cut meant that this couldn't happen and it was difficult to feed and entertain a disappointed, tired little girl by candle light before getting her ready for bed.

The year after the end of my marriage to Glenn was very sad and very very lonely but in retrospect it was also a very creative time in terms of remaking myself. As ever I turned to books to get me through the lonely hours and most importantly discovered Doris Lessing's 'Golden Notebooks'. As a consequence I began taking my own scribbled notes more seriously and, though I didn't know it at the time, like my genetic mother before me, began keeping a more regular notebook to contain my feelings.

When Glenn first moved out to stay with our friend Nancy I was not sure what the situation was with his new love affair. He had told me a little more about her, that her name was Sian and that she was a primary school teacher but I didn't know how serious their relationship was. Glenn was not the sort of person to talk about his feelings let alone his plans, so I decided to speak with

Sian. I phoned her and invited her over for an evening to talk. When she arrived she was smaller, prettier and younger than I and seemed very confident though doubtless she wasn't. We treated each other gently, drank lots of wine and talked.

What really broke me up, although of course I didn't show it, was her casual, confident and unthinking use of the word 'we' whenever she spoke of her and Glenn. Each time I heard it, was like a knife in my soul and sealed my doom. I managed the meeting and I suppose learnt what had to be learnt and although I agreed to meet with her again it was a long while before I could do it. I poured my pain and anger into my notebooks and in doing so not only managed to contain it but also took hold of it. Reading my notebooks back to myself in the cold light of dawn I found myself wondering why I was taking out all my anger on Sian? Why was I not angry with Glenn as well but kept going on about how much I loved him?

The prevailing Women's Movement of the times was an enormous support in all of this and, as so often happens when relationships crash, I turned to my female friends. Amongst them was Elli who was a very radical feminist. Under her influence I joined a women's poetry group where we read established women poets and shared our own writing. Elli was a Canadian film-maker who lived alone and had a little boy about the same age as my daughter. In many respects we were the forerunners of what would become an increasingly normal role for women and young girls in the years to come, that of the single mother. We used to sit and talk at my kitchen table while our children played 'mummies and daddies' beneath it. There was one glorious moment when we were talking good, strong feminist talk and my daughter's voice suddenly piped up from under the table as she said to Elli's son "you can be the daddy and drive the car and I will cook dinner". Elli and I looked at each other and then rocked with laughter; it seemed there was a long way to go.

I shared my notebooks and my feelings about Glenn and Sian with Elli. We talked about how, as women we dance to the man's tune and how easy it is to always blame the other woman when things go wrong. We wanted to reject this because we didn't want to sound like bitter, disappointed women. We wanted to like and love our men yet ideologically we wanted to be on the woman's side. In these talks I found that if I was a reasonable human being and admitted to liking Sian then I grew angry with Glenn for hurting me and it was destructive of me because it seemed to negate all that had been good in our relationship. But when I owned and admitted the passion of my love for Glenn I felt so hurt and angry towards Sian that it was destructive of me and my values, my need to be a better person. On top of that my greatest concern was to protect my daughter and soften any pain of loss she might feel over her Daddy leaving us. I knew I had to try and find a third way and decided to very slowly and carefully try to find a balance so that no one would get hurt.

Under the influence of the 'women's movement' and my resulting need to be pro-female; along with my hippy tendency towards 'peace and love' I decided that the only way forward was to try and be friends with both Glenn and Sian so that all of us could become a kind of extended family and my daughter would not have to make painful emotional choices. Maybe Sian felt the same way because she made the effort to befriend me, never undermined my role as Shoshannah's mother, and her wider Welsh family welcomed my daughter into their midst. My own parents were unhappy for me and I know my Mother was very worried. She knew instinctively how hard this was for me but always backed me up and supported me in the position I took.

When Glenn and Sian moved in together I agreed that Shoshannah would spend alternate weekends with them. Every other Saturday I walked with my daughter in her pushchair, through Waterlow Park and across Parliament Hill Fields to what was now Glenn and Sian's home. I hated that moment of arriving at their basement door but they always invited me in. While Shosh settled down we grown ups drank tea and talked about how she was getting on. I have to admit that I felt increasingly jealous of their warm little family unit especially when Sian became pregnant with their future son. The Writer's and Reader's Publishing Project which they had started was also becoming more and more successful and as it did so they moved further into the intellectual world of Camden Town and Hampstead.

With the birth of their son they were no longer a couple but a family and consolidated it by buying a bigger flat closer to Sian's married brother and his family. They appeared more and more to be a 'proper' family and Shosh was always a part of it. She had holidays abroad with them and hero worshipped her Dad as we all did for he was a very charismatic and lovable person. I hung around the fringes of all this and perhaps, because being on the fringes was such a natural place for me, I may have allowed myself to go there too willingly. I went there by choice but it badly affected my relationship with my daughter in that it undermined my confidence in myself to be a proper mother. Family and belonging has always been an immense problem for me and now it felt like I was failing in my ability to create my own family for my daughter. Never was this more evident or more strongly felt by me than in our arrangements for Christmas.

We agreed that Shosh would have every alternate Christmas with Glenn and Sian so that she could be a part of their little family and also have shared time with her half brother. We are told relentlessly, that Christmas is a time for family and this is difficult if you are a single parent with only one child. On the alternate Christmas Shosh and I went to my parents since just a mother and a child hardly constitutes a family. It also gradually happened that I would be invited to the Glenn and Sian family Christmas as well so that I would not be on my own and would not miss having Christmas with my daughter. I did this for many, many years until my daughter was grown up and had children of her own for whom she provided Christmas and a family for me. Once again I could do it because I knew how to be an illegitimate member of a family but I always hated it and Christmas for me meant my failure to be a proper Mother and provider of family for my daughter.

I had to wait until I was in my seventies to finally get over this feeling of failure. By then my daughter's father had died as had my second partner. On the spur of the moment because she was exhausted from work and her partner had also recently left her, my daughter phoned to ask if she and my grand children could come up to me for Christmas. Of course I was thrilled and said yes but was simultaneously plunged into anxiety as to whether I could do it properly. I rushed out and bought a small Christmas tree, some fairy lights and a few strings of red and gold tinsel. Then to the supermarket to buy the stuff of Christmas dinner; meat, veg, Yorkshire puddings, along with Christmas pudding, brandy sauce, ice cream and crackers. And it all worked out just fine. We cooked together, ate together, gave presents, played a silly board game and slumped in front of the TV. It was low key but lovely and I felt that at last I had managed to be a proper person with a proper family that was all mine and for whom I could properly provide.

Despite the anxieties that the break up of my marriage to Glenn confirmed in me and the affect it had on my relationship with my daughter, I have come to be very proud of what both I and Sian achieved. We both worked hard at finding a way forward and at being friends. A few years after our break up Glenn and I got divorced so that he and Sian could marry. The divorce took place at the High Court on The Strand, not far from where Shoshannah had been born. It was very equitable since neither of us owned anything and mostly involved our agreed arrangements for Glenn's role in Shoshannah's life. Afterwards we went to the newly opened Cranks vegetarian restaurant and had lunch. I never stopped loving Glenn but with time I moved that love to another place. And most importantly my daughter and her half brother have a real close and loving relationship based on the shared experiences of their childhood.

When Glenn became ill with cancer in his early sixties our daughter nursed him through the final stages. By this time his marriage to Sian was also over and he'd had a third relationship and another daughter with another woman. Both Sian and I tried to bring them into our extended family that we had worked so hard to create but she was not willing to join us. Maybe the era of 'peace and love' was just too far gone by then but when Glenn died we were all there; his children and his grandchildren; Sian and myself together at his bed side to say goodbye.

9

Walking on the Wild Side

My job at the Media Resource centre had helped to stabilize me in my sorrow and because the job was part time I had more time to be with my daughter and my women friends. My life seemed to settle down into an easier rhythm and I became more confident and happy with myself. What I didn't know was that I was about to meet my soul mate and slip into chaos. My daughter got chicken pox and I had to take time off work to look after her. At the end of ten days, when she was no longer infectious we were both bored to tears with being cooped up in the flat. We needed a trip out somewhere so I decided to go and visit Stephen who had been designated as Shoshannah's godfather and was always pleased to see us both. I had no way of getting in touch with him but I knew his address in Hackney.

I found him sharing a house off the Queensbridge Road with a guy called David who had got the use of the house from the Acme Housing Association. The house was old, run down and completely bare of furniture. Stephen introduced me to David, who was a Jewish, slim hipped, electronic engineer with lots of wild curly hair. With an almost courtly bow he offered to show me round the house while Stephen disappeared to make the tea. The stairs and landing were bare and empty and my daughter rejoiced at the noise her feet made, filling the house with echoes. The door of the front bedroom was shut "that's Stephen's room" David said. "This is mine" and with something of a flourish, he pushed the opposite door wide open. The first thing I saw was a mattress on the floor with a saucer for an ashtray beside it along with an old, battered Golden Virginia tobacco tin and a packet of green Rizlas. "How do you like the wallpaper" he said, with a sweep of his hand. I saw that two walls were completely covered with what appeared to be old maps. They were not coloured maps but black and white. "They're old nautical navigation charts" he explained "We found them in the basement. Look" he pointed excitedly "you can see the Straights of Formosa here in this corner" I didn't know how to react so I turned to look for my daughter who had disappeared. I pushed past him and hurried downstairs where I found her in the front room with Stephen who had dragged out a couple of old boxes, a cardboard tube and an old tennis ball for her to play with.

David set about lighting a fire in the small, cast iron grate in the fireplace and we sat on the bare floor in front of it to drink our tea. He took out a tiny cube of hashish and held it into the flame of a lit match. With an air of formality he laid the Rizla papers end to end, sprinkled them with the loose tobacco, crumbled in the softened hashish and gently rolled a spliff. With the elegance of a craftsman he rolled a neat roach and twisted the other end. "Do you smoke?" he said, offering me the spliff as though it were a plate of dainty cucumber sandwiches; needless to say I was enchanted. We sat and talked while Stephen played with my daughter. Somehow or other the conversation came round to books and he launched into his love of James Joyce's Ulysses from which he could even quote long passages. He seemed so erudite and yet he spoke with a strong East London accent complete with much 'effing and blindin' which completely entranced me. David later confessed that he was equally enchanted by me. He thought I was an actress because of my long hair, my croaky voice and the way I waved my hands when I spoke. He told me about his love of flying; that he had a private pilot's license and because he was hopeless at navigation he called himself 'White Knuckles Airlines". He made me laugh but I didn't believe him. "Take the day off work" he said "and I'll prove to you it's true. I'll fly you to Brighton and we'll have an ice cream by the seaside" and I agreed to go.

A week later on my day off from work and after I had dropped off my daughter at nursery, he took me first by underground then the overground train to a small airfield on the outskirts of London. The sun was shining and a warm wind was blowing through my hair as we strode across the airfield to a small two seater plane. I felt so free and lovely and as though I was in a James Bond movie as he strapped me into the seat behind him, powered the engine and then we were up and away. What I hadn't realised was that small planes don't fly very high so looking down I could see a patchwork of fields and strips of red roofed houses. It made me feel sick so that I had to shut my eyes and grip the arms of my seat until we landed.

He helped me out of the plane, smiling with delight "Let's go find some ice cream" he said. I looked about me, desperately trying to control my shaking knees. We seemed to be in a field in the middle of nowhere. I focused on the scarlet windsock stretched on its pole while I tried to get my balance. David pulled me towards a small control building that stood on the edge of the field "What ice cream do you like, chocolate or strawberry? I've got enough money to get you one" he said, rattling the loose change in his pocket. But the flight had blown away my feeling of being a free and lovely young woman. Standing there in the middle of an unfamiliar field I felt unhinged and didn't even know if I liked ice cream let alone chocolate or strawberry. My hysteria mounted as we struggled across the field to the control building where I saw to my horror that it was already 4.45pm. "We can probably get a ride to the beach" he said taking my hand but I pulled back crying "Look at the time! look at the time! I have to get back. The nursery closes at 6 o'clock. I have to get back to my daughter!" On the flight back he called out "I think we are lost! Keep your eyes open for a railway line" But I couldn't look down. I shut my eyes, aware only of the fact that I was completely in his hands. I would have to trust him to get me home. Which of course he did and it wasn't long before he moved into my home.

My daughter was still going to Glenn and Sian's every other weekend so David and I would have those weekends together. It had been hard, working and being responsible for my daughter on my own for almost two years, so my weekends of freedom with David were a great release. We used to make love, smoke spliffs, eat cream cakes and all the time talking and sharing and growing closer and closer. But of course there is a difference between being lovers and living together and he wasn't just moving in with me, he was moving in with my daughter as well. Shoshannah and I had just had two years of being alone together, coping with Glenn's absence and looking after each other. I found it hard to let another man into my domestic life where, as the father of my daughter, Glenn still seemed to belong. I still felt related to him in that way and Shoshannah loved and hero- worshipped him. David had also been married and had two children of his own whom he still saw regularly so, in the school holidays, they joined mine and Shoshannah's life as well. It was all too much, too soon and we all of us handled it badly. David and I decided that maybe the three of us, myself, him and Shoshannah needed to go away somewhere new together so that we could set up our new relationship.

On one of the weekends when Shoshannah was away at her Dad's we spent a crazy evening with a map of the world, a felt tipped pen and a few perfectly rolled spliffs. We began to score countries according to the likelihood of them producing happiness for David, Margaret and Shoshannah. As each country failed to come up with the required meeting of needs we scored it out with the felt tip pen until all that remained was Canada. So that is where we decided to go. I took out all the money I had in my superannuation pension scheme to buy tickets and I handed in my notice at work. I was thirty four years old and after fifteen working years I finally stopped being a librarian.

I packed up my stuff at the flat and took anything that I cared about which included a rocking chair, my books and an old oak chest of drawers that I'd had in my first flat in Islington and was the first piece of furniture I had ever bought, and arranged to leave them with my sister who was now married and lived in Swanley. Everything else I left behind for Glenn to clear up. We were going to have to stay at my sisters for a couple of days before our flight so David arranged for two Hoxton friends, Will and Arthur, to take us and my stuff to my sisters in a big old van. On the way there they seemed very nervous and both attributed this to them having to travel South of the river which, they assured us was a big thing for any one coming from the North side. Halfway there we stopped for petrol and it was only when we scurried furtively away from a parked police car that I cottoned on to the fact that the van had probably been nicked. It was my first step onto the other side of the law and it would not be the last.

We had arranged to fly to Toronto and stay with my first love Peter who was now separated from his wife and had his teenage children living with him. It may have seemed a strange choice but I had remained close to Peter and he had moved from being a lover to a father figure for me. When we arrived at Toronto airport there was some kind of hiatus. It appeared that two planes had arrived together so the place was unable to cope with what, for Toronto at that time, was a seething crowd of passengers. As a consequence we just walked into Canada. Although we held our passports open for inspection nobody came forward to look at them. There were no barriers and, more to the point in terms of our future, nobody stamped our passports with an entry date or a visa. We became illegal by accident and we didn't even know it.

My former lover had offered his home to us as a place to stay out of love for me and a sense of responsibility towards me, but living there was not easy for any of us. There was increasing tension between him and David; my daughter was disturbed and unhappy and behaving badly; and I just floated between them all never quite knowing whose side I should be on nor what to do. We had no plans and were making it up as we went along. Then I met a librarian who worked in the Toronto education system. He wanted to use the PRECIS indexing system and had been looking for someone for over a year to help him. As I was trained in it he promptly offered me a year's contract to work with him. We had only intended to stay in Canada for a few months but this seemed just too good an opportunity to set ourselves up in a new place and stabilize ourselves so I applied to Canadian Manpower for a work permit. We felt very sure that this would be granted since I plainly was not keeping another Canadian out of work.

We were so confident that we let our return tickets to England run out and, while we waited for the work permit we decided to visit my Uncle Gerry who lived on the other side of Canada on Vancouver Island. My superannuation pension funds were running low so Shoshannah and I went by train and David took the bus. At that time the Canadian trans-continental train still ran and when it pulled out of Toronto I had a terrible feeling of panic which lasted for about fifty miles. The train carried me into its own momentum as for four days and three nights Canada rolled out beneath us and I began to feel very calm. Shoshannah had no interest in this great, wide world outside the train window. She played with her dolls in the space at the front of the carriage near the drinking fountain. As usual she chattered away to herself and her English accent soon enchanted enough passengers for her to be petted all the way across Canada. Meanwhile I stared out at miles and miles of passing land and felt nothing. It was only in the middle of the endless, flat prairies that a kind of claustrophobia took hold of me. So much space, yet I felt landlocked, desperate for the edge. I became aware of my Englishness, that I was an island person and needed to arrive at the sea after a day's travel. Canada just seemed to go on and on, and then there was the terrible shock of waking up on the last day in the middle of the monstrous and overbearing Rockies.

Gerry Gosley met us off the train at Vancouver where our legs felt wobbly to be on firm land again. He lived on Vancouver Island where he had worked since the end of the War for the British Tourist Board running and performing the 'Gerry Gosley Smile Show' and he was very camp. We got on the ferry boat to the Island and watched hundreds of beautiful tiny islands float by us under a purple evening sky. Amidst all this beautiful strangeness the first thing we saw when we got off onto the Island was a No.11 red double decker London bus and the town of Victoria had a distinct feel of Eastbourne about it. That said Gerry lived in a beautiful house on the side of a hill overlooking a bay. In the evening we could watch the lights of the tug boats as they silently hauled logs from one side to another and in the day we walked on the shingled beach littered with sun bleached, sea washed, silvered logs. It was idyllic but very unreal. David had arrived the day after us completely disoriented by his ride across Canada where the guy next to him on the bus had shared his cans of coke which he had laced with vodka to make the journey more bearable.

Gerry's house was filled with theatrical mementos and we had to listen to a great many tapes of his shows whilst he mixed us manhattans regardless of the time of day. After a week he took us to his cedar wood cabin which was in about four acres of virgin pine forest. Here we sweated, naked in his hot stone sauna, we ate black Alaska cod and Gerry kept up a constant supply of manhattans. We stayed there while David helped Gerry build an extra room onto the cabin and I kept Shoshannah amused and safe since there were wild bears and it was too dangerous to let her go far. It was so remote and quiet there that you could almost hear the silence. I also knew that we were running low on money and needed to get back to some sort of reality. So after what can only be described as a surreal two weeks we flew back to Toronto feeling sure that my work permit must have come through by then, but of course it hadn't.

We had very little money left but we we found a tiny flat above a doctor's surgery in the Italian quarter of Toronto. It was a bargain because it was over a Doctor's surgery and in return for a low rent and free heat David had to service the boiler in the basement and I had to clean the surgery reception area. We had no furniture just a double mattress for me and David and a single one for Shoshannah that we bought at the Salvation Army Warehouse for ten dollars. Tuesday night was garbage night in Toronto, when everybody put their rubbish out on the sidewalk for the garbage men to collect. We began regular hunting trips and found a piece of carpet for our room along with a few pots and pans for the kitchen. But the real find was a large box of odd lengths of material put out as garbage by a furnishings shop. All the material was new, bright and pretty. From it I made pillow cases for our bed and new blinds for the windows so it began to feel like we were putting a home together.

David got a job working illegally for an Asian guy who had his own electronics company and if we were careful we had enough to live on. I was concerned about Shoshannah who had reached school age but I wasn't sure about getting her into the state school system since I was becoming increasingly worried about our status in Canada. My former lover came to my rescue and payed for her to go to a private school. The head teacher was a lovely Yorkshire woman and the teaching staff were either French Canadians or English teachers who at the time were not easily accepted into the state schools. It was very gently alternative and bi-lingual with the staff teaching and talking in whatever was their natural language be it English or French. Shoshannah's class teacher was French so her first experience of school and first school report was in French. Then I saw a job advertised in the local super-market for someone to iron two mornings a week at the Divine Decadence Boutique. This was owned by a couple from Birmingham who sold antique clothes mostly bought in England which they then laundered and sold. For three dollars an hour, two mornings a week I ironed lovely nineteen thirties lingerie in powder blue satin or peach crepe de chine whilst smoking a joint or two. The couple who owned the boutique belonged to an alternative Canada and knew craft people. I began making patchwork covers out of my box of coloured scraps which kept me sane while I worried about the work permit, but also thought they might provide me with a ticket into some kind of alternative community. However, my inability to decide which side of the fence I wanted to stay on was once again going to be my downfall.

The job offer as a PRECIS indexer was still hanging in the air so I got in touch with the Manpower people in Canada to try and find out about my work permit. They were very curt with me and told me I shouldn't think I was special just because I was English and I should wait my turn. This undermined my confidence a little and since I didn't want anything to go wrong with the work permit application I did what seemed the logical thing to do but turned out to be really foolish. I went to see the immigration officer to regularise our position and extend our visas not realising that because of the chaos when we entered Canada, we didn't actually have visas. In fact nobody knew we were in Canada and the immigration officer was extremely suspicious. David and I were summoned for an official interview where we explained what had happened at the airport. We had never had any intention of being illegal and the mistake was all theirs.

Of course there was no way the immigration officer was going to admit that the State of Canada might have made a mistake. We were grilled as to our motives for being in Canada and he implied that we had deliberately and illegally crept in over the border. He then gave us twenty four hours to leave voluntarily otherwise we would be deported. As we came out of his office I noticed a long line of Asian men, women and children waiting in line to see the immigration officer as we had just done. I felt so strongly for them because I knew what was waiting for them in that office and more terrifyingly I now also knew what it was like to be outside the law and have no rights We thought we would have to be deported since we didn't have money for a flight but my ex lover bailed us out again and bought us return tickets to England. It was just before Christmas when we left behind our little flat with its patchwork quilt and blinds and with just two suitcases and fifty dollars to our name, got on a plane for England.

We thought we were going to Canada to sort out our relationship but I'm not sure that we did. When we set up our little apartment in Toronto we worked hard scrubbing it clean, arranging our minimal furniture and making it home. The first evening there David made spaghetti Bolognese, we were after all in the Italian quarter of Toronto, and I spent some of the remains of my pension fund on a bottle of wine. We were supposed to be celebrating but in truth neither of us felt like it. For my part I was filled with nostalgic memories of setting up home with Glenn and wondering why I was doing it all over again. We were very quiet and have since admitted that we both felt what was almost an anti-climax within each other. But the details of our future were all there in that evening; David cooking, fixing things and making me laugh; me worrying about money, my daughter and our future; along with both of us feeling uneasy about setting up home. That pattern never left us for another thirty five years but we could never let each other go.

10

Back and Forth to Nottinghamshire

When we got back to England we had two suitcases and fifty dollars. We went first to David's parents who lived in a tiny council flat not far from Heathrow and the next day I went with my daughter to my parents who now lived in Devon. We had decided that we would go to wherever either one of us found a job and of course it was me. I found a job as a school librarian in a large village in South Nottinghamshire. Initially we lived in a very damp and very cold flat in the City of Nottingham. I travelled out to work by bus each day and David was responsible for taking Shoshannah to a school close by in the City. It was while she was at this school that we became worried because Shoshannah kept asking us what 'a dirty Paki' was because she had heard the children saying it in the playground. We immediately made an appointment to see the Head Teacher who tried to assure us it was just silly children's talk and meant nothing. When we protested and wouldn't let it go she got increasingly angry and was almost shouting at us as she said "they come here because they love us, they love our way of life" which was pretty horrifying but pretty much in line with the prevailing attitudes of the day.

Meanwhile we had made friends with Steve who was a sociology teacher at the school where I worked. He was left-wing and like us believed in an alternative lifestyle. He owned a run-down terraced house in a village much closer to the school where we both worked. The house needed re-wiring and plastering so together the three of us planned that David, Shoshannah and I would go and live with him. In return, David, who was not just very clever but could fix almost anything, would carry out the work on the house. When that was done we would sell it and get a bigger house where we could live as some kind of alternative community.

I moved Shoshannah to the school in the village and Steve was able to drive me into work with him. For the long hot summer of 1976 the plan seemed to be going well. David re-wired and plastered; we dug over and planted the garden with vegetables and David built a small polythene covered lean-to on the back wall of the house where we grew tomatoes and marijuana. I was also working closely with the English teacher at school and between us we set up a whole school poetry week with lots of extra curricular activities all revolving around the Library and poetry. We had Ivor Cutler come up and delight the children with one of his crazy performances and we hooked up with the local radio station to broadcast a daily poem written and read by one of the children in the school.

Our hippy bubble burst when Steve fell in love and got engaged to a girl who did not share our counter culture dreams and was very keen for her and Steve to have the house to themselves. Over the months things got increasingly tense and eventually Steve saw the folly of his ways and asked us to leave. Our falling out was very bitter and we found ourselves homeless in a rather posh little village that just had a small row of shops and one bus an hour into Nottingham. It was also impossible for me to get to work since I could no longer get a lift with Steve and there were no buses that went that way. In my search for a solution I noticed that one of the shops in the village appeared to have an empty flat above it and I enquired if it was available. The people who owned the shop lived in a large house and used the flat for storage but I managed to strike a deal with them. They wanted someone to work in the shop and they also wanted a cleaner for their house. In exchange we could live in the flat. In desperation I left my job at the school and accepted their deal. David and I found ourselves moving into a tiny flat with bare floorboards, very little furniture and only one open coal fire for heat. The stress was infectious and we very quickly had a massive row which resulted in David packing his things and heading back to London where at least he would have a chance of finding work.

Left alone with my daughter I was viewed with considerable suspicion by the inhabitants of the village which was very much a commuter village filled with well-heeled families from the professional classes. They couldn't quite place me, a middle class single lady with a brown daughter living above the shop where I served them and cleaned for the shop owner. The other mothers at the school gate were very reluctant to talk to me when I picked up Shoshannah. I felt I had lost my footing, fallen off the edge and I knew that things couldn't go on this way. I needed at least to get back to where I would be more acceptable and there would be more chance of finding proper work.

The only support that I had was from the English teacher who had worked on the poetry week with me at the School. I had remained friends with him and his partner and it was him that suggested a solution. He had a friend who taught in the American Studies Department at Nottingham University. Apparently it was a really exciting course and he suggested that I apply to get on it. Although I was a Chartered librarian I had never been to University and at this time it was not only free but there were generous living allowances available. It seemed a way forward so I applied and was accepted onto the degree course. Now all I had to do was get back into the City.

I discovered that there was a housing Association in Nottingham City called Family First and that it provided flats for single mothers. Some of the flats were custom built and gathered around the Association's Family Centre but they also had others in converted older houses in the surrounding streets. I applied and managed to get one of these on the ground floor. Shoshannah and I were able to move back into the City and my poor daughter started at yet another school.

At Family First I was a middle class mum amongst mostly working class young women. But we were all single mothers who had many of the same needs. We baby sat for each other and spent long hours talking and sharing over cups of tea and a cigarette in whoever's kitchen was available at the time. It was a great set up and I made life long friends during the two years that I lived there. The other great thing about Family First was that after two years you become eligible for council housing so I eventually moved to a large council maisonette on an estate just around the corner. This also gave me a spare bedroom and I offered it rent free to one of my fellow students at the University in return for her helping me out with my daughter, such as collecting her from school if I had a late lecture. Liz rapidly became a member of the family and I couldn't have done my degree without her support. It was a time when I felt very strong and secure in myself and my daughter had some continuity of home and school which made her a happier person. All this time David was in London solving his and eventually my housing problems by setting up a Housing Co-operative with a bunch of our Hackney friends. He and I would meet on the weekends either in London or Nottingham and avidly share our lives whilst my daughter was able to see Glenn and Sian on the alternate weekends that I spent in London. It was an old pattern for us that we never truly valued nor recognised as the one that worked really well.

In London David had earned some money by doing building work for Tariq Ali at the Islington offices of the IMG which was the British, Trotskyist section of the Fourth International. One summer whilst he was staying with me in Nottingham we met a guy called Keith who introduced us to the Nottingham branch of the IMG called Big Flame and which David always referred to as Little Flicker as there were very few of us. We went to some very dull meetings where we talked political theory and 'the way forward' whilst David and Keith began planning an alternative, radical radio station. One weekend I took my eight year old daughter to a Socialist Challenge, fund raising, children's party. It was held in a bleak, defunct church hall on the St Anne's council estate. The hall was decorated with bunches of balloons and there were tables with paper plates, jelly and iced buns. We fervently believed in liberation, so the children were allowed to do what ever they wanted in the name of freedom and it was horrible. Pumped up with sugar the children grew wild, burst all the balloons and soon began throwing food at each other. Without boundaries some inevitably turned to fighting whilst others clutched their mother's skirts and cried.

This was my contribution to my daughter's experience of liberation informed by socialism. But on the other side her father was able to give her an entirely different experience. Through his publishing co-operative he had become close friends with John Berger who that same summer invited him, Sian and our daughter to his place in France for a holiday. So my daughter spent a week experiencing the world of socialist ideas on the sun filled meadows of the French alps whilst the grown ups talked over a glass of red wine. This glaring gap between what I was able to provide for my daughter and what she experienced with her father added to my deep sense of failure as a mother.

My consolation was that I was not only enjoying but also doing really well at my studies. I was at the stage of writing my dissertation which could be about anything American. David and I talked about it at length and eventually I chose to write it on the development and use of the electric chair. I chose this because it was uniquely American but in the course of my research I discovered its close relationship to the late nineteenth century, anti-capital punishment movement in New York, and the battle between Edison and Westinghouse over a system for distributing electricity. It was a successful dissertation and as a result I was offered financing for an MA which I could do at either the University in Nottingham or at the Institute of American Studies in London.

Faced with a decision I once again made it for all the wrong reasons. I still wanted to be what I thought a proper person should be and that involved trying to be a proper family with David even though our relationship worked really well when we didn't live together. So I chose London, went to live with him in the Housing Co-op and of course it didn't work out. Neither David nor I were equipped to be husband and wife and we soon fell apart. This involved me moving to a succession of temporary homes within the Co-op and my daughter was quite plainly becoming increasingly unhappy with every move. So I left the Co-op, gave up my MA and my Marxist belief that 'property is theft', and returned to being a librarian in order to be able to buy somewhere permanent to live. Shoshannah was approaching secondary school age and was failing badly largely because I had dragged her from place to place and school to school in pursuit of my own happiness. I felt so concerned for her plus immensely guilty. I bought a little terraced house in Forest Gate and promised her she would never have to move again which she didn't until she became a mother herself.

At secondary school she never really recovered from her unsettled and fractured early education. To my everlasting shame she went to six different primary schools and with a librarian for a mother and a publisher for a father she refused to be interested in books. She left secondary school with very few qualifications and, unsurprisingly rejected any ambitions her father or I might have had for her. My relationship with her in her teens was the standard battle of wills but enhanced by my own inability to know what was the right and proper thing to do. Unlike me she made her choices with a fierce determination and by the time she was twenty one she had found a partner and had two children.

I loved my daughter dearly but that love was always underpinned by my old fears of loosing her love if I didn't do things properly. I felt and knew the love between us but was never able to trust it. It was through my grandchildren that I came to finally not just know, but trust in the bond of unconditional love. I was there when my grandson was born and held him when he was less than five minutes old. His little brown eyes looked up into mine and I remember vowing to myself that I would always let myself just love him and never do anything out of guilt or more importantly, the fear that I might loose his love. My grand daughter's birth was difficult and she was in the Special Care Baby Unit for ten days. Waiting with my daughter, through that agonizing time I made the same promise to myself.

They are grown up now and we live many miles apart but we talk on the phone at least once a week; they share bits of their lives with me and they visit me. They have been not only a gift but the balm that has healed the wounds of my own beginnings and tipped over into a healing of the relationship between my daughter and myself. Their father also did not stay with them so I played quite a large part in supporting my daughter in bringing them up and providing for them. She has always said that her children grounded her and after having them she went back to college to do an access course then a degree course to become a teacher. Ironically, given her childhood relationship to books, she has become passionate about literacy and the role of real books in early education. I am immensely proud of her and more importantly, I have learnt to relax in the knowledge of the love between the three of us. We do not live close to each other but we are a family.

Throughout my time at the Hackney Housing Co-op and Forest Gate I was working as a librarian at Homerton House which was a boys secondary school in Hackney. East London has always been a hub for new immigrant communities and in the eighties London was opening its doors to the global community. There were twenty seven different languages spoken within Homerton House School and tension was rife. There was so much potential for conflict between the Afro-Caribbeans and the Africans, the Turks and the Greeks, the Chinese and the Vietnamese and the English who seemed to hate everyone. None of this was helped by the fact that the School was housed in an ugly, seven story high concrete block of a building and, being a boys school was filled with teenage, male testosterone.

The Library became a place of refuge for the boys who couldn't handle the playground and I had a fleet of library monitors many of whom acted as translators for me. I bought books in many of the languages spoken in the school especially the Asian languages since that's where the demand was. Through my library monitors I learnt to visually distinguish the scripts of Punjabi, Bengali and Urdu even if I couldn't translate them. One of my most constant monitors was a year seven boy called Mohammed whose family were from Egypt. For a small boy he had many responsibilities. After school he had to pick up his sister from nursery and buy the family's supply of fresh pitta bread on the way home. Then he had to go to mosque for prayers and only then get down to doing his homework.

It was the time when the fatwah was issued against Salaman Rushdie for bringing out 'Midnight's Children'. A debate was raging and one day I asked Mohammed what he would do if he found the book on the library shelves. He looked up at me with his serious little face and said "I would burn it Miss" and we smiled at each other. I became very fond of him so when he didn't appear at school for three weeks I went to his home to see if he was alright. His father showed me into their run down little flat above an equally run down shop in the market, and explained that Mohammed had been off school with the chicken pox. He showed me into the sitting room and told Mohammed to go and fetch tea for his 'teacher' which he did and dutifully brought it to me on a small tray. Mohammed's father told me that he was an academic and involved in a research project at the Imperial War Museum yet they lived in such humble circumstances. The flat was poor and sparsely furnished but I felt it to be imbued with a coherency built on a kind of care and respect that seemed so missing in the increasing cacophony of the Hackney streets.

I worked at the school for almost ten years but was finding not only the school but also the journey to work more and more stressful. In the mornings the station at Forest Gate, where I had to get the train to Hackney Wick was so packed with people that I usually had to wait for a couple of trains to go past before I could get on one. My walk from the station to school involved walking through the church yard which was always a tiny moment of peace. One morning I got on the train and was jam packed up against a man who stubbornly held his newspaper with his arm crooked so that his elbow was in my face. By the time I got to my station I was so cross that when I got off the train I deliberately stood on his foot. Later as I walked through the church yard I felt so ashamed. It was only eight thirty in the morning and I was already stressed and wound up. As I had these thoughts I noticed that I was kicking the dead leaves on the ground with real childish pleasure. It made me realise that Autumn must have set in and I hadn't even noticed. I was so out of touch with the natural world and it felt like a sign that it was time to leave London.

David was also living with me by now partly because he had been doing up my house and partly because he had lent his Housing Co-op flat to Shoshannah and her little family. She and the children's father had been renting a house privately but were made homeless when the house was re-possessed because the owner failed to pay the mortgage. Eventually and with a lot of struggle she managed to get housed in temporary accommodation by the council but in the interim David lent her his flat and moved in with me. So now I owned a house, had two lovely grandchildren and my partner was not only living with me but doing up my house as well. It should have made me feel secure but my relationship with David never worked well when we lived together. I was also now beginning my menopause and one of its effects was that I had times when dark clouds of depression seemed to drop down on me without rhyme or reason. I felt increasingly inadequate and that I was failing in my efforts to do the right thing and be a proper person.

All of these things contributed to my leaving London again and for the first time in my life I was the one doing the leaving instead of hanging on and waiting to be left thus confirming my worst fears about myself. David and I were a fatal combination. We came together physically and intellectually with an equal passion. We were truly soul mates and nobody has ever quite known me as David did. We knew each other's minds and bodies so well and so intimately but we could never quite find a form for our relationship. I needed to get out on the edge again where I always felt safe so I ran away from everyone and everything.

In 1989 I applied for a school librarian's job in Sutton-in-Ashfield on the outskirts of Nottinghamshire and took it because I still had friends there from my Nottingham days at Family First. I sold my house, which upset both my daughter and myself and went alone to the Midlands. The School I was to work in was in stark contrast to my London school as most of the children were English and white. In London I had been used to such a medley of faces that at first I found it difficult to tell one from the other amongst this sea of white faces. Many of the children came from the neighbouring village where the pit had recently closed as a result of Thatcher's battle with the miners and was very deprived and run down. But there was also something very private and self sustaining about the village and its children. It was as though the Country had dispensed with its labour so they had quietly turned their back on the Country and faced inwards.

Soon after I started working at the school a service was arranged at Westminster Abby to pay respect to the contribution that the now ex-miners had made to the Country. The Grimethorpe Brass Band was to play there and Archbishop Runcie performed the service. Two children in every school in the mining communities, which included ours were invited to the service. I volunteered to be one of the adults who accompanied the children down to London and it was amazing. I sat with the children in the Poets Corner and cried as Runcie praised the miners and the Abbey filled with the glorious sound of the brass band. Outside the Abbey when we left we found Ted Willis and Arthur Scargill being mobbed by the children for their autograph as though they were pop stars. Initially the children at the school saw me as a foreigner but it has to be said that my southern with a touch of London accent gave me a kind of kudos along with the fact that I brought a bit of the wider and more urbane world with me.

As a school librarian I belonged to neither the Office staff nor the Academic staff but contributed to the school from somewhere in between which not only gave me considerable autonomy, but is the place where I have always felt very comfortable. Now that I was in a less chaotic school I was able be creative and give the library a strong role both within and off the school curriculum. Working at this school was very good for me. My sense of being an outsider began to take on a positive role. It no longer under-mined my self confidence but actively contributed to it. The Midlands became not just the place I had gone to in order to be alone and feel safe but a place where I actively chose to be and remain. That said, I was dreadfully lonely and missed David enormously as he did me. We kept in touch but only by phone.

For the first three months in Nottinghamshire I lived in a hotel that mostly serviced the needs of traveling salesmen. But the two gay guys that owned the hotel were very sweet to me and always had a glass of red wine waiting for me when I got back after a day's work. In the evenings I sat in my room, watched TV and knitted jumpers for my grandchildren until I managed to rent a converted old barn for a couple of years. Maybe we were looking for an excuse, but we arranged for David to drive up with some of my furniture which he had been looking after. Once again we began our merry-go-round of being together yet not able to be together. He began to stay with me, sometimes for weeks on end and I was still making regular trips to London to see my daughter and grandchildren. In spite of all our experience and maybe because, when we were together it was so good, we still hung on to a dream of living together.

For three years we tried to find a place for that dream by driving all over the Midlands looking at all sorts of odd places and spinning dreams about what it might be like to live there. As ever, this exercise was underpinned by the familiar tension of David's need to take a risk and live dangerously which I loved in him because it made up for my own need to feel safe and in control. Eventually I found a small house in a village in the coal fields of East Derbyshire where property was cheap enough for me to buy. David came with me but once the adventure of the search was over he was soon back in London as he had never given up his place in the Housing Co-op. If I am honest with myself I was also glad that he would be there, keeping an eye on my daughter and her children whom he also felt to be his grandchildren. Once again we slipped into the pattern of long distance relationship which seemed to be the only one that really worked for us but it had moved on. Although I was lonely, it was me who had chosen to move away and, although I didn't really recognise it, I was beginnning to accept that it might be better this way.

11

Ancestor Hunting

Soon after my move to the Midlands my father had a serious heart attack and my sisters and I gathered with my mother at his hospital bed. He survived the heart attack but was seriously weakened so we sisters stayed on for a couple of weeks until my father was out of hospital and settled back at home. My parents were long retired and had moved back to my mother's hometown in Norfolk. One afternoon, while my father rested, I drove my mother and two sisters to Kimberley where her grandmother had been born and lived. It had once been a small rural settlement with a church and a handful of tiny, thatched cottages for the farm workers. Now the cottages had been repaired, painted varying shades of pink and cream and served as second homes for middle class commuters.

It was a lovely, soft, English summer day filled with sunshine and a bright blue sky. We rambled in the cemetery amongst the nettles and tilted gravestones with my mother looking for ancestors. She found her grandfather and a great aunt along with various other names that she recognised but didn't know what relationship she had to them. As she searched my mother wove stories of her childhood memories, pulling my sisters and I into a shimmering web of family history.

It was a special day. Apart from anything else it was the first time for many years that we three sisters had been home together without our respective husbands, or partners. My father's heart attack had been a first shock wave of impending mortality that called us together before it was too late. My eldest sister had brought a notebook with her and as we searched the gravestones she wrote down significant dates. She wanted to get it all down while our parents were still alive. I was a part of this lovely day but felt myself increasingly on the perimeter, on that edge that defined my inclusion and exclusion. It had nothing to do with my place in the family. It was history that put me there. The lovely day belonged to me as much as it did my mother and sisters, but the history was not mine. The sunshine and nettles were mine but the names on the gravestones bore no relationship to me. The further back we went in history the more I felt myself receding so that I was both there and not there.

When we returned home filled with the soft day and happy family thoughts the mood continued. Now my father was drawn in as over the tea table and into the shadows of the evening he told us tales of his family. I felt myself faltering as it got harder and harder to pretend that I belonged to all this. I felt increasingly like an interloper but I didn't want anyone to notice. I didn't want to spoil this lovely day with my uncomfortable truth. I felt that if I stayed and said nothing I was making a mockery of it all but if I left I would bring the day to an awkward halt. Like the bad fairy at the christening, whichever way I looked at it I had only an evil gift to contribute. I wanted to just disappear so I feigned a need to go the the bathroom and went upstairs.

I had of course under-estimated my mother who soon followed. She sat next to me on the bed and hugged me tight. She said how sorry they all were. How I was so much a part of them, such an absolute part of the family that they had forgotten. She dried my tears, I cheered up and a little sheepishly rejoined the fold. But the fact remained that they had forgotten as they always did and I had not forgotten as I never could. However much they loved me and I loved them I couldn't forget and this inability made me feel so much less a good human being than they were.

We didn't know then, but my eldest sister was right in her instincts. There was only going to be one more time when we would all be together in my parent's house. Two or three years later and again in the early summer, my mother had a series of minor strokes and then a massive one which left her in a coma, halfway between death and life. We three sisters gathered again, this time at my mother's bedside in the hospital. We did not know if she could hear us but it seemed she might. For a week we sat around her bed and recounted the rosary of our childhood memories that were so important to her until she quietly passed away.

My father had become too frail to keep the house going and had arranged to go into residential care. After my mother passed away we stayed on to arrange her funeral and help my father sort out the stuff that he wanted to keep with him in his new home. The rest we would get rid of. In such a situation family history could not be avoided. This time it came to us in a small, old, battered brown leather suitcase that was bursting with family photographs. We could not throw them away so we three sisters sat on the floor one evening and divided them up. The festive family occasions, the marriages, the new homes, the new babies, visiting relatives. Our childhood unraveled before us. School photos, summer holidays, Christmas gatherings. We had shared this history and knew which was important to each other so the dividing up was easy. The hesitation came only as we moved back into the past, to the faded sepia records of the previous generations. There were fewer of them and they were all the more precious for that. It was that summer's day in Kimberley all over again except this time my sisters did not forget. They offered me the photographs of the great grandparents knowing they had nothing directly to do with me. And I refused them gently, knowing how precious they were to them.

It was a good evening in which we had wordlessly recognised something and managed it well. I felt so secure in my sisters' love and unspoken acknowledgment of me and my history that something became free inside me. I knew that I had to do what my sisters were doing and gather up my own history before it was too late. But my feelings of guilt, that I might be betraying the people who had loved and nurtured me still held me back. I had told my parents about that first meeting with my genetic parents and after that, whenever I went home my mother often asked me, hesitantly and almost shyly, if I had seen them again. I always hastened to say no, to assure her that they were not important to me, that they meant nothing to me. Saying this to my mother may have reassured her but not as much as it reassured me. It made me feel like a good girl who was doing the right thing and as a result firmed up my position, my belonging to the family. So I didn't take up or couldn't take up my search for my ancestors until my father died and I knew for sure that I couldn't possibly hurt them; a fear that came from me and not them. I didn't have long to wait as my father lived for less than a year after my mother died. I now felt free to take up the search for my past that I had begun all those years ago.

That first meeting with my genetic parents had felt so brutal this time I protected myself and began with the paperwork. All I had on paper was a short form of my birth certificate which simply gave my date of birth and my adopted name. I also had a copy of my adoption papers dated two years after my birth wherein, stamped, sealed and at a price of 7/6p the child I was born was changed to the child I became. It was this original child that I wanted to know about so I decided to try and get her full birth certificate. I was lucky in my search because at that time the records of births, marriages and deaths were all housed at the Family Records Centre in Islington. Sadly this has now closed down and the records are only available on request through the mail or Internet. At the time I first visited it there appeared to be no computers just open book stacks that held, in chronological order, the large ledgers recording the three main events of our lives, red for births, green for marriages and black for deaths. In this beautiful simple way all the records for over a hundred and fifty years, from the registry offices all over the Country were gathered in and made accessible to the people and families to whom they belonged. It was such a user friendly place and there was considerable public anger when it finally closed down in 2008.

On the day I first visited there must have been over a hundred people there, all busy ancestor hunting. We moved quietly around each other, respecting each other's privacy, although I felt very curious to know what my neighbours' search was all about. The floor was carpeted and the only noise was the soft thump as the ledgers were pulled from the shelf and opened up onto the smooth, oak book rests. All that was needed was an approximate date and then a steady finger to run down the columns of names recorded on the much thumbed velum pages. I found the red volumes that covered the year I was born, pulled down the one that covered the last quarter of that year and ran my finger down that part of the alphabet that covered my original surname.

Starting this search had felt like stepping into an empty space at the centre of my identity. A space I had always acknowledged but until now had always pushed to the margins. I felt so excited and then so dismayed when I found my name wasn't there. For a minute I felt like I didn't exist but then discovered that the records for adopted children were, like virgin births, in separate white volumes. I steadied my finger to begin my search again and there it was! My original name with my mother's maiden name beside it and the place where my birth was registered. So much information so quickly and so easily. All I had to do was fill in a pink form with the record number and a brief account of why I wanted it, pay a fee of seven pounds and they would send it to me.

The birth certificate arrived through the post a week later and when I opened it I felt so substantial. There it was, my original self written in pen and ink, dated and signed by the General Register Office. I was a real person! I returned to stare at that birth certificate again and again and each time it provided more evidence. There were details of my father and his occupation along with the full name of my mother. It was thrilling and there was no stopping me now. I returned to the Family Records Centre with enough clues from that birth certificate to find both the birth and marriage certificates for my original parents and from them for my grandparents. When they arrived through the post there was a second extraordinary shock. I found that the house where my original mother was born was in the street opposite the school where I was presently working. Not only that, the address on my mother's father's birth certificate was in the next village from the one I presently lived in! How could such a coincidence have occurred! I had always thought that my genetic parents were from Helmsley in Yorkshire where I was born but her birth certificate told me she was born here, where I now lived, on the borders of Nottinghamshire and Derbyshire. The certificate also told me that her father, my grandfather was a miner so I assumed he must have moved here for the work.

I spread the certificates out on my kitchen table and felt like my own particular soap opera lay before me. Names, places and dates that hinted tantalisingly of relationships and domestic dramas. When I began this search for identity I thought it had to do with genes and the need to know who I looked like, but now I had a history that stretched beyond the present and into the past. Moreover, by complete accident I appeared to be living and working where much of it had begun. For the first time in my life I felt a very real and comforting relationship to the past. However, there was still the present to deal with.

So far the search had felt very safe and I wasn't yet ready to change that so I returned again to my paper evidence. This time I looked more closely at the little brown Post Office savings book made out in my new name and with my original name crossed out with Post Office red ink. In the past I had focused on this seemingly such easy change of name and hadn't bothered to look at the surname and address written beneath from which fresh evidence now sprang to life. The address on the book was the same as one mentioned on my birth certificate so the person who had opened the account was someone close to me. The surname was not mine but it was an unusual name and the same as the names of the witnesses on my birth parents' wedding certificate. So I had a name and address that had to have meaning.

Just as I did for that first search all those years ago, I went to the public library and looked up the name in the telephone book for the appropriate area in North Yorkshire. There were three of them listed and one was still at the address in my Post Office book. Back at home I looked at my collection of certificates on my kitchen table and at the phone number I now held in my hand. The first contact I had made with my birth parents had been by letter and felt much slower. There had been time between each communication for my emotions to settle and for me to get some kind of control over them. Now it was simply a question of picking up the phone.

When the phone was answered I asked for the name of the person in my Post Office Book. The woman on the other end of the line sounded cross and explained that she only rented the property although it still belonged to the family of the woman I asked for who had passed away. My heart sank as it seemed like the trail was quickly going cold. I realised that I would have to give a little more if I was going to get any more. So I explained to this complete stranger, this voice on the other end of a phone, that I'd been given away as a baby and my search for my past had brought me to her address. Now she opened up and told me that although the old lady was dead her son, who owned the house, was still alive and lived in the same village. She told me to hang on a minute while she got me his address and that she knew he was away on holiday for a week.

So I wrote to this man and explained my connection with the house he owned and the fact that his surname appeared on my Post Office Savings book. About ten days later he phoned me and in his solid, open, Yorkshire voice told me his name was Dan and that we were indeed related although he couldn't quite work out what the relationship was. What he could say for sure was that he was my mother's cousin. I asked him if he knew about my mother's children and he told me that he had met her daughter who had twin daughters herself. This of course was not me but the daughter my parents had told me of at that first meeting. I sat on the other end of the phone as he scattered names and relationships before me. I tried to scribble notes lest I should forget but I was bowled over and breathless. He pressed an invitation on me to visit whenever I liked as he had photos he could show me.

David had been involved in and encouraged and supported me in this renewed search. He now suggested that we drive up to my birth place in Yorkshire and take up the invitation to visit. So we drove up to Helmsley which was by now quite an up-market small town. I stood before the row of small, now gentrified terraced cottages where I had been born but in all honestly didn't feel anything very much. Dan lived in a new bungalow on the outskirts of Helmsley and welcomed us with open arms. His wife was also a local woman and they had a small shop on the market square. She had obviously been putting out feelers amongst the older locals and told me, with some relish, that although she met people who knew my mother, nobody knew that she had ever had a child whilst she lived there. Dan showed me and gave me several family photos that went back through the generations but he was not sure who they all were. Finally he gave me a phone number which he said was either my mother's or her daughter's. He wasn't sure which but knew that the two of them lived close to each other in Somerset.

It was a good visit and on the drive home my head raced with the information he had given me. I had thought that my genetic parents might be dead by now, but from Dan I knew that my mother at least was still alive and he had raised the reality of my genetic sister whose existence had always stayed unresolved and increasingly fanciful in my head. All those years ago I had promised her parents not to let her know of my existence and I didn't want to break that promise but genetically at least, she was undeniably my sister. Once again I held a phone number in my hand that would bring the past racing into the present.

12

Sisters and also a Brother

There is something very particular about the relationship between sisters. You may be very different in temperament and even looks but you grow up together. I had two sisters, one on either side of me. For most of my life at home I shared a bedroom, that most intimate of places, with my youngest sister. Initially we shared the same big double bed with the iron bedstead on which I used to tap tunes when I couldn't get to sleep. My eldest sister had a tiny bedroom of her own but on the weekends when we didn't have to get up for school, she would come into the big bed with my little sister and myself and we all giggled together. I have to say that it always puzzled me how my eldest sister managed to worm her way into the warm spot and I usually ended up outside on top of the bed larking around and making the other two laugh. It is a moment that defines our relationship; the bossy eldest sister, the compliant youngest and the middle one, an entertainer to the others.

Later on when my parents were wealthier and had a bigger house, my youngest sister and I still shared a bedroom with matching divan beds and a chest of drawers each. But we learned to move around each other protecting our own and not invading each other's space. My eldest sister still had her own room until she left home to get married which was when I inherited it. But before that I used to sneak into it and try on her dresses and shoes. Indeed it is in that room that I learnt to walk in stilettos! This is my experience of sisters although we shared not one drop of common blood. Even now, in middle age, living miles apart and within our own families we remain sisters. When we talk on the phone we laugh at the same things and we call upon our shared experience to support our opinions. There is so much explaining that we don't have to do because we each know where the other is coming from. Even when our opinions diverge love and loyalty softens our responses to each other and ensures that we try to understand each other. There is such a dense relationship packed into that small word 'sisters'.

I also have a brother who was adopted into the family later in my parents' life and after my eldest sister and myself had left home. My mother had gone back to work as a nursery nurse in a children's home and quite simply came to love one of the little boys. At first she just brought him home for weekends until finally she and my father adopted him because they loved him enough to want him to be a proper part of the family. His experience was very different from mine since he was four years old when he came into the family and had experienced several foster parents. My youngest sister probably has the closest sibling relationship with him because she was still at home when he came into the family and so she shared more family life with him. My eldest sister was by then married and had her own children and so her relationship with him is more an act of choice, almost like an arranged marriage made out of loyalty to my parents since she had no experience of shared childhood nor of living with him. Once again that fearful word 'choice' enters the equation as to where one may claim or be claimed, not to be loved since that is never in doubt, but where one belongs. I am somewhere in-between because, like my eldest sister I didn't experience living with my brother. But he and I share our adopted status which provides an unspoken bond between us. I know how important it is to both of us to prove that we are both legitimate members of this family and to support each other in that belief. I don't know how easy or uneasy my brother feels within the family as we have never talked about it. This may seem strange as we have the experience to share but demonstrates what a fearful territory the whole business of belonging can be for children and parents alike.

So what of this other sister, the full-blooded one with whom I shared nothing except a full set of genes? I was in my early twenties when our shared parents first told me about her and at that time I could not handle the knowledge of her. I was hurt by the fact that our parents had not only given me away but also hidden my existence. But I couldn't dismiss her and she had lived in my head for more than thirty years. In my imagination she was always a thin young woman walking alone down an empty road and I have to admit that I came to enjoy the power that I had over her. After all, she did not know about me. She did not know that a dark and ugly creature lurked in the shadows of her life. A creature with the power to shake her sure knowledge of herself as the only treasured child of loving parents who could not bare the thought of loosing her. Sometimes I imagined stepping out of the shadows; crossing the road to meet her; declaring my presence; insisting on my existence. If I am honest, the feeling warmed me. She was the daughter they kept and loved.

I was banished to the dark whilst she walked in the sunshine, innocent and unknowing. I felt like a bad person who nevertheless had the power to change everything but I didn't. The fact that I did not hurt her when I so easily could; that I protected her from the frightful creature that lurked in the dark made me feel better about myself and somehow less evil. But perhaps the time had come for me to get her out of my head and make her real.

The pressure to find her also came from the reactions of other people, as well as from myself. Now that I no longer lived near my sisters, new friends would ask if I looked like them and increasingly, as I and they aged the answer had to be no. When we were young family mannerisms, ways of being and talking, allowed people to think we looked alike although we always knew that we didn't. It is surprising how often when meeting a new family people immediately look for likenesses. We were three little girls who quite frequently, especially when we were dressed for best to meet strangers, wore matching dresses. Our presence would be greeted with words such as 'Oh don't they look alike' and then perhaps the strangers gaze would move to the parents with words such as 'well they take after their father or mother don't they' or 'well you have your mother's eyes don't you'. When this happened my sisters and I would smile inwardly and knowingly, enjoying the truth of the matter and the delusions of these adults. But although I enjoyed the collusion with my sisters it did always leave that little troubled question in my mind 'Who do I really look like?'.

Now that my sisters and I live apart with families of our own, and as we have grown older, we have aged differently both in physical looks and style. In contrast to me, my two sisters are more like each other than I am to them. They both have hair which has turned to the same kind of silver as our parent's. My eldest sister keeps hers lightly permed whilst my youngest has hers carefully cut by a hairdresser. I have kept my hair straight and never visit a hairdresser. I have not 'gone grey' let alone silver apart from a couple of streaks at the front and I have kept my hair long in a plait. My sisters would probably say this has more to do with choice of style than genes but it would seem that with age, genes become a little more insistent.

Now that I was older I found the question of 'who I looked like' once again becoming relevant to me. One of my strongest memories of that first meeting with my genetic parents so many years ago, is of searching their faces for likeness. I noticed that I seemed to have my father's hairline and most definitely my mother's nose and eyes. It is that nose and those eyes that I see in my own daughter so I can detect a bloodline stretching into the future, and have seen it in the recent past, but what about the present. This unknown sister was of my generation so what did she look like and did we look alike? I did not want to break my promise made all those years ago but I had a phone number burning a hole in my hand. I was so involved in my own needs that I gave no thought to what awful memories I might be opening up on the other end of that phone:

> *How many more surprises is life going to throw at me. I have almost come to dread the ringing of the telephone. This evening my darling Margaret got in touch. That tiny, dark haired little scrap that at just six weeks old in 1939 I had reluctantly agreed to part with. The memory of waiting at York Station for the London train which was full of troops on their way to war. The sound of Margaret crying when I handed her over still cuts my heart like a knife but it had to be. Nothing will ever ease that pain. I do not remember much about returning home with empty arms and my aching heart. But life continued from that time onwards. Hal and I remained loyal to each other for 52 years but it seemed as if we could never bare the pain of opening our hearts to each other about Margaret and we never mentioned her.*

If I had known all this I may never have made that phone call but I did. A woman's voice answered my call and since I was not sure who it was I asked if I could speak to Anne, which I knew to be this sister's name. She asked "Who am I speaking to" and I didn't know what to say. I just stammered out "I think I may have made a mistake and maybe I'd better write to you" All this with no introduction of myself. "Could I ask who I am talking to?" She repeated. "Well, my name is Margaret..." I began, but she interrupted "I think I know who you are" she said and then "Listen I am at my mother's house at the moment. Can I go home and call you back from there" which I agreed to even though I was afraid that she might not call back.

But she did and it was the first of three excited phone calls during which we exchanged the surface of our lives. I asked her how long she had known about me and she told me only since last year. Apparently our shared mother's sister had also had a child which she had given away. A boy, now a man who last year came looking for his mother. But he was too late since she had died so he visited them instead. She told me what a sad day it was and after he had gone her mother told her about me. I did not ask her how she felt about that sudden revelation and I realise now, in light of the way our relationship has progressed that it was a missed moment.

She has since told me how her whole reality did a shift that evening when she picked up the phone. And later she told me in an email how she has found it difficult to come to terms with the enormity of my existence. It shook everything she knew to be 'true' about herself and she was still trying to work through all that. But I was so locked up in my own responses that I totally neglected her and her reality. Instead the conversation bounced excitedly along the smooth surface of exchanged information. Information in which we sought to make a connection with each other by looking for similarities. The fact that we both had straight, brown hair, both had daughters, both were divorced. Finally we agreed that we should meet up in London that being equi-distant from where the two of us now lived, and we could stay with our respective daughters. Hers' lived in Hackney and mine in Forest Gate so we decided to meet at the Museum of Childhood at Bethnal Green. In retrospect this sounds poetic but in reality was just a convenient halfway between the two.

The closer I got to the projected meeting the more uncertain I became about myself and what we might talk about. I wouldn't be able to talk about my family because that might seem hurtful and a betrayal. I couldn't talk about my life as I didn't want to show off and I didn't want to be the big sister who had done it all before her. I got there early and waited on a bench in the pale Autumn sunshine. I felt formless, and could not feel my outline. I had no idea of what self I was about to present to this person I was meeting. But I knew it was her as soon as she came through the gates and began to walk along the curved gravel path towards where I was sitting. As she approached I stood up and took a few steps towards her. But she did not give me time to greet her. As soon as she was close enough she put her arms around me and hugged me, squashing my face into the fur collar of her coat. We stepped apart and in that awkward silence she took the initiative and suggested a coffee. We walked into the museum and sat opposite each at a table in the cafe.

We did not quite know what to say, where to begin, but we kept looking hard at each other. Were we truly sisters? I guess we were both still looking for likeness and she told me how much I looked like my mother. This must have been very strange and maybe disturbing for her but once again I was so locked up in myself that I failed to respond to her experience and allow her space. For some reason I found the fact that I looked like my mother very consoling. I had after all, begun this new search with 'who do I look like' in mind. At some point I wanted to touch her, not hold her hand, not hug her, just touch her skin to find out if blood mattered? Would something resonate between those two skins. I touched the back of her hand and I think I expected a kind of electric shock, a tingle of recognition as that same set of genes kept apart all their lives, now came together. But no, the recognition was of the mind and not the body. My eyes saw the character of her skin, it's colour and its texture; my brain recognised a similarity but it was not felt.

We finished our coffee and went outside. We walked round and round the little square beside the museum, enclosed by iron railings and with the wet, fallen leaves of the London plane trees stuck to the pathways. We talked and talked and as we talked we disclosed. It was a cautious disclosure and one I suspect we had both rehearsed. I also discovered during this sharing of history that I didn't know which personal pronoun to use when referring to our shared parents. When referring to my original parents was I to use the word 'our mother and father' since that is what they were, biologically speaking, or 'your' mother and father since that is what they were for Anne whilst for me 'my' parents were the ones that had loved and nurtured me. It may appear trivial but to some extent this simple confusion and uncertainty over a personal pronoun contains the whole relationship which this 'sister' and I had yet to unravel. I don't know how difficult it was for Anne but it certainly raised huge questions of love and loyalty for me.

As we talked, Anne gave me her version of things which she had learnt only recently from her mother and I gave her mine which I had known all my life as told by my parents. There was of course a discrepancy not in the facts, but in the emphasis. The two sets of parents had experienced the same event from opposite sides, one giving and one receiving. The difference in emphasis lay in their reasons for telling the tale. My natural born parents had given their baby away and then hidden that fact from their second natural born daughter for more than forty years. Indeed the father of this baby went to his grave with the tale untold. It was the mother who told the tale to her second daughter and then only because circumstances forced the issue. So her version was a justification and in that telling she also shared a little of her mother's pain and guilt which must have been enormous. So to some extent Anne's telling of this tale was underpinned by the need to defend and protect her parents. I on the other hand had always known my story, had grown up with it. It was told to me by choice since my parents believed it was better that I knew the truth of my beginnings right from the start. The context for their telling of the tale was always to make me feel good and loved. So there was this difference in the tale we told as we walked round and round that square. Anne was telling me how her mother finally explained how hard it was for them, that the war was on, that they were so young, how the family gave them no support etc. And she was right, they had had a horrible time. But I felt an increasing anger. I wanted no excuses, no justifications, it disposed of me too easily. I wanted to express this anger but I was too polite, too uncertain and I let the moment go. During one of those first phone calls Anne had said that she didn't just want to be a 'go-between' between her mother and myself and at the time I didn't understand. Only later did I come to know what she meant, that she wanted me to know her for herself. She was right of course, but for now it was all about me.

We did not talk about how she must have felt on hearing the news of my existence. I don't know if that was out of her need to protect her parents or because I didn't give her that space to talk about herself. It was a missed opportunity since this was just the beginning of our only bit of shared experience. If we were to have a relationship perhaps it should have begun there, with us sharing the differences but we let the moment slide away. We went for a drink in a nearby pub but it was desultory and the pub was horrible, full of working men knocking back beer in their lunch hour. In retrospect I think we were both so determined to make things right, to honour all the decent and loving responses that well brought up middle class, middle aged women should have, that we overwhelmed the situation with a determined niceness. That is why it all felt so unreal and why the pub with its awful reality was too much for us. We both agreed that we didn't know what to do with this relationship but since it existed, at least in flesh and blood, then we couldn't quite let it go. Before we parted Anne invited me to visit her at her home in Cheddar and I readily agreed. But in retrospect we had different agendas. Anne had said that I didn't know anything about her and that she wanted me to know her for herself. For my part there were still things I wanted to know about myself and I wanted to meet my mother again before it was too late since I realised she must be getting old.

A few months later I took the train to Bristol where Anne met me and drove me to her flat which was only ten minutes walk away from her mother's home. We were still quite distant and careful with each other and I know from later emails that we were both dealing with complex and quite angry feelings. Anne has since told me that she was angry with her parents for keeping me from her, denying her a sister and for my part I was angry at being kept hidden like a bad secret. As well brought up girls, we kept this anger to ourselves. It was our first shared experience as sisters but we were not yet quite sisters and so not yet quite ready to share it.

When she picked me up at the station I asked Anne if she had told our mother, Mildred, about my visit and felt very shocked when she told me she had but Mildred was not sure that she wanted to see me. Once again I was making this meeting all about me and my needs forgetting that there were other people involved in all this who also had needs. We spent what remained of the morning swapping information about our daughters and mostly just looking hard at reach other. In the afternoon Anne suggested a walk to show me Cheddar but I was still concerned to see my mother. So I asked her to show me where Mildred lived which she did and then I asked her to leave me alone and I would find my way back.

I walked up to the bungalow and knocked on the door. When Mildred, my genetic mother, opened the door it was almost as if she was expecting me. We didn't speak, just hugged each other and she showed me into her sitting room. We sat on the sofa, held hands and she talked to me not so much about the circumstances of my birth, we had been over all that, but about her marriage to my father Hal and how awful his death had been. He had a violent stroke when she was alone with him in the house and she had to call first a doctor and then an ambulance to get him to hospital. He was completely incapacitated by the stroke but she wanted to look after him herself so she brought him home. There followed days with him calling for her from his bed and then not recognising her when she came. Instead he was angry and sometimes lashed out at her, even bruising her face one time. The two of them were alone together when he died on Christmas Eve. But she was proud of their marriage and the fact that they had stayed loyal to each other for 53 years.

She told me how alone she felt when he died and as she told me she reconnected with that other most painful time in her life when she had to give me up. This was when she told me how she had written down all her pain and had a shoebox full of what she called her 'scribblings'. She added that she didn't know what she would do with these scribblings, that she ought to make a bonfire and burn them before it was too late. The thought of that horrified me, for they contained my history as well, so I asked her not to and if she ever wanted to get rid of them maybe she would send them to me. It was a moment when I felt very close to her. I wanted to embrace her as she sat there in her loneliness but I couldn't. Even as I felt her pain my love for my adopted mother rose before me and I could not betray it. It was Olive's love for me that had filled my dark soul with light. I never had to go to her, she always stepped into my darkness and took me in her arms insisting on loving me regardless of my genes. However, the scribbled notebooks, so like my own brought me close to Mildred. She was my inherited, genetic self and she filled my heart with shame and guilt. I felt as if I'd reached the nub of myself, the real me. The me of flesh and blood not choice; the me that if you stripped away performance brought only darkness and sorrow. What I didn't know at the time and should have known was that it was as difficult for her as it was for me:

> Its a lovely bright, frosty, sunny day and I sit here not knowing what to do. Part of me would love to see this daughter who was only six weeks old when we parted, on the other hand part of me is almost afraid of all the old memories coming back. Wondering if after all these years maybe it ought all to be left alone. What is it going to achieve other than a lot of heartache for everyone. Life has moved on, I no longer feel the strong bond that is between mother and child.
>
> The door bell rings and on the doorstep stands a middle aged woman which I instantly know is Margaret. The resemblance to myself is unmistakeable. There were no words said we just put our arms around each other whilst the tears flowed. So maybe I was mistaken and now know that whatever happens and however many

years go by that strong pull of a mother's love is always there. It was strange meeting her, like meeting my other half as she is so like me in so many ways. Maybe she has now filled the need that she so obviously had, maybe she will keep in touch, who knows. I no longer ask myself these things. I have so few years left now and just would like not to be hurt anymore

Before I left Mildred showed me a painting that she had done of Helmsley where I was born and she showed me a framed family tree that she had made with family photos that did not include me. Then we walked back together to Anne's place where all three of us hugged. A mother and her two daughters together after almost sixty years. But I suspect Anne felt the same as I did and we hugged each other for the sake of our mother. She was an old lady who needed some respite from the pain that had informed her life. It was a second act of unspoken sharing for Anne and I, another step into the shared history that we were beginning to create.

When I got home my two sisters who knew about this visit, almost immediately phoned me to see if I was alright as they were worried for me. I let their loving concern wash over me and was glad to be back in the arms of this family of mine; to come once more out of the dark and into the light. I told them a little of what I felt about the meeting with this other family but out of my own need to feel secure I slanted my account towards reassuring them that this other, dark family meant little to me. Out of a sense of loyalty that they did not ask for, I assured my sisters that I had no need to meet my mother and this other sister again. But that was not quite true even though I worked hard at believing it.

Another thing that happened as a result of this visit was that in looking for my past I now had an unintended vision of my future because I did indeed look just like my mother. On my return home I kept catching a glimpse of myself in the mirror and seeing my mother. My thickening body and the set of my head on my shoulders was just like hers. I had got used to not looking like anyone and found it very liberating but now I had a picture of my physical self as an old lady and I didn't like it at all. I continued to send regular Christmas cards and birthday cards to Mildred and when Anne and I parted we assured each other we would keep in touch, which we did with a certain ambivalence. We tried to keep the relationship going through uneasy emails but we did not rush to meet again. I left her with an open invite to visit me but she did not take it up until many years later.

13

Breaking and Making

I turned sixty and retired as a librarian as we moved into the next millennium. A year before I had been with a friend to an exhibition of City & Guilds Creative Textiles student work which was lovely. I decided there and then that was the life for me so after retiring I signed up for the three year course. As a woman, especially one who had grown up in the fifties, textiles was an easy choice. I was taught to sew a fine seam at primary school and as a teenager, before the days of cheap Chinese imports, I frequently made my own skirts and dresses. I was also already exploring my ability to sew a little more creatively. David was an electronics engineer and like me scribbled his thoughts and dreams in notebooks. Unlike me, his notebooks were full of circuits and diagrams. We both found printed circuits very beautiful and David always said that there was an aesthetic in science as well as art. So long before I took up creative textiles I had begun to embroider his circuits onto calico in rainbow coloured silk thread. The City & Guilds course was techniques based which was wonderful but more importantly it taught me to look at the world in a different way and see its patterns, shapes and colors.

By the end of my three year creative textiles course I had discovered the art of making felt from raw, combed wool and I went on to take another three year course in doing just that. Felt is one of the earliest of fabrics and there is something very elemental in the making of it. The transformation of raw wool into a material that can be manipulated, dyed and shaped is a journey but in the final process of heating and shrinking one never has total control. Felt is an adventure because what is produced is always the result of a tension between what the maker wants and what the felt is prepared to do. I made and dyed felt with wool from sheep reared in the Orkneys, that had been fed entirely on seaweed. Having made this felt I stitched, steamed, rolled and pleated it to make as many varieties of felt seaweed as I could. At times the felt took control and I allowed it to express the cold, grey seashores of the North Sea. As a result of this, and much to my amazement I was invited to have an Arts Council supported exhibition of my work on the Isle of Mull. David drove me up there and we had a wonderful week full of the wild beauty of Scotland including a romantic stop-over in a bed and breakfast on the shores of Loch Lomond.

David was my mentor and my technician and he told me I was his muse. He was by now living in a small apartment in the village next to mine where he continued to work and invent within the world of electronics. We saw each other most days, especially for what we called our early morning 'rants' where we raged at the increasingly awful behaviour of the world around us. We went for long walks in the wild Derbyshire Peaks and sometimes we stayed over with each other. It was good and we seemed to have found a way of making our relationship work.

It looked like I was becoming an artist yet, as ever I didn't feel myself to be legitimate. I had never had any art education and I didn't know how to behave as an artist. So I took a course entitled 'Continuing Professional Development' to find out how to be one. For the first lesson we were given a long, thin, willow stick, an easel with a large sheet of paper and a pot of inky black paint. Before us was a still life arrangement of large, leafy plants and we were told to draw it using the willow stick and black paint. It was terrifying and eventually totally liberating. After a life time of believing I couldn't draw I found out that drawing began with making marks on a piece of paper.

During the course we were also taught and given an opportunity to practice various kinds of print making. Dry point printing grabbed my attention largely because my grandson, who was by now in his early twenties and doing a BTEC in Art, showed me how he had been using the technique. It consists of drawing with a hard steel point into a soft metal plate. Once a mark is made it cannot be erased so it spoke to the side of me that wanted to be a risk taker. On the other hand, printing the plate once it has been inked up is meticulous. It needs clean hands and a careful alignment of the damp paper onto the plate ready to go under the print roller so it appealed to the librarian in me.

As I moved from cloth to paper it was perhaps inevitable that I returned to the world of books which had not only provided me with a living but sustained me through much of my life. I wanted to find a way of bringing the word into visual art and vice versa. Not as description but as an integral part of any piece so that they were two sides of a single response. I also did not immediately give up on felt. I began a project which resulted in a library ladder made by David out of beautiful tulip wood and upon which I made and placed hand made felt books with thin white felt pages that fell down the ladder as the books gradually disintegrated. The felt words spelling 'Once Upon a Time' gradually became separate letters which fell off the pages.

My second major project came as a result of my experience at the Family Records Centre. It consisted of an open fronted cabinet, once again made by David with lovely hand cut, dovetail joints. I silk screened my birth and marriage certificates onto fine white felt, rolled them and strung them in the cabinet on red legal tape fixed at the top with red sealing wax. I made similar folded felt documents, silk screened with my adoption and divorce papers, tied them with red ribbon and placed them in a small drawer within the base of the cabinet. I called the project 'Autobiography' because it described my personal narrative. At the Family Records Office I had so strongly felt the tension between the fact that we are born into an empty free space and then almost immediately documented. On the one hand it seemed such an intrusion into our personal freedom and yet the sustained effort of the documenting was so impressive. Had it not been carried out we might never have known from whence we came.

Books were becoming my metaphor but I wanted to deconstruct the form of them and use it to fuse the visual and the written word into a single artistic response. I was of course still keeping my own notebooks as I had always done and now I turned to them as a source of inspiration. Apart from my outpourings of angst, they were full of a lifetime of snippets both prose and poetry some of which I had worked on and some just written at the moment of experience. I enrolled in a summer school at Bristol University to learn how to make 'artists' books' and began to make little books in every conceivable form using both my dry point print skills, my creative textile techniques and words from my notebooks. I began to exhibit these books at small town and village art festivals; contributed to artist book exhibitions in places as far apart as Wakefield and Basingstoke and took part several times in a National Artists' Book competition and exhibition.

But I still didn't think of myself as a bona fide artist. I knew that much of my success was down to my ability to perform, to put on a good show. I always wanted to believe that really and truly I was a writer. Writing things down had always been my way of getting hold of things, shaping them and in that process making sense of them. My little books were a first step into bringing out some of my writing, disguised as art, into a public space. But writing was my way of making up the missing narrative of myself and I couldn't risk finding out that was all rubbish. David was my only audience and his love of my writing always reassured me that I was a real person. So it was the most terrible shock when quite of the blue David disappeared one day.

I did not hear from him for several days and no one seemed to know where he was. I had a key to his place but when I went round there was no sign of him. Finally he phoned me and told me that he had gone to live with another woman in Nottingham. I was stunned as I had no idea that he wasn't happy with me. Looking back on it I can see that we were both having to deal with encroaching old age and the changes in our physical relationship that came with all that. I was re-channeling my energy and finding expression for myself through my art activities and had neglected to see that although David was totally supportive of me, he was increasingly feeling diminished by his sense of getting older and loosing the best of himself. His reaction to this was to find and make love to another woman. That sounds dreadful and I am sure he also liked his new woman but during that first phone call to me, by way of not so much an explanation but more of a justification, he told me how surprised he was to find how much he had got left in him and I could hear the vigour that he could not keep from his voice. He told me that she was a child psychologist who lived in a large house in a very wealthy part of Nottingham, that he had got to know her over the Internet and decided to move in with her. Later he told me that she took him shopping to buy him clothes and shoes which felt very bizarre. David had always been a one t-shirt and a pair of jeans man so I felt he was betraying not just me but who he was and our way of life as well.

However he did not stop phoning me almost every other day and he kept asking me if we could stay friends. At one point in time I was to exhibit at an arts festival nearby and he turned up on the first day as a surprise, with lovingly prepared sandwiches and a flask of coffee because, as he said, he knew me so well and rightly knew that I would not have prepared any for myself. But I was devastated and broken inside. In the evenings and sometimes in the small hours of the morning I would walk round to his place in the next village in the hopes that the lights might be on and he would be there, which he never was. As the months went by I continued to answer his phone calls and talk to him about ideas and politics as we had always done. He wanted to make a web site for me and my work which was his excuse for phoning me and mine for answering him. But really I was just hanging on and it was tearing me apart. One day when I couldn't stand the hurt any longer I went to Nottingham and the posh, gated community where she and now David lived. I didn't know the exact road nor house number but I walked the streets of huge old Victorian houses until I found David's car parked outside one of them. I just stood there and stared at it and then was violently sick on the pavement. My head throbbed and I couldn't really work out where I was or what to do. I remembered that my best friend from my Family First days worked in the Council Offices in the middle of the City so somehow or other I found my way there. I must have been a strange and distraught sight but the doorman called her up on the internal phone to come down to me. She took one look at this sobbing, shaking creature and said nothing. She just took me into her office and made me a cup of tea while she packed up her work and then took me home. I knew I was in trouble and could no longer cope so the next day I went to my doctor to get something to help me sleep and she recommended me to a counsellor who turned out to be brilliant.

Once a week I sat in the counsellor's room and after I had cried, she slowly drew me into taking a close look at my relationship with David. How he was being very cruel to me but I was also complicit. What we were doing to each other was a more extreme version of the dance we had regularly done around each other throughout our life together. In that dance my role was to hang on out of an intense need to prove that it was impossible to leave me. David, for his part new exactly which buttons to press to set the dance in motion so that he could both leave me but also know that he would not lose me, that I would always be there, hanging on. My counsellor related this back to my origins and my deep fear of being not so much abandoned but as being un-chosen. We talked about the lengths I would go to in order to prevent this happening and that it might be at the root of my need to be constantly reassured that I was a 'proper person'.

The fear of being un-chosen has led me to always hover just beneath the top line and rarely put myself forward to be first choice. It has kept me sitting on the edge; never quite coming down on one side but keeping one foot firmly in each camp. In my personal relationships I hang on, always trying to respond primarily to the needs of the other person so that it is almost impossible for them to un-choose me. I have frequently written about this feeling in my notebooks and how my behavior makes me feel I am a dishonest and evil person but I have never spoken about it. My counsellor now encouraged me to do just that and more importantly to recognise and value that early experience of being chosen so that I could understand that I didn't have to try and be one kind of person or another in order to be worth keeping. Nothing changed over night of course, but I grew stronger so that one day, when David phoned me, I finally had the courage to own all of my feelings. I told David that I could no longer talk to him because it was too painful, that I was definitely saying goodbye and I put the phone down.

I had already been in touch with a close friend who now lived in Somerset so as soon as I put the phone down on David I packed a bag and drove off to stay with her for a few days. My friend lived very close to where my genetic sister lived so I also arranged to meet up with her one afternoon. I was probably too emotionally fragile for this meeting but it was my way of pushing myself so that I felt strong and could handle anything. Anne and I met for a drink in a local pub and hugged each other like sisters might do.

But even though we shared a full set of genes we were still strangers. We did not talk about the past since we had already gone over all that. Anne told me that 'our' mother was getting physically frail and might soon need sheltered accommodation. I think that for us both, it felt like this shared, sad mother of ours stood between us and kept us apart as we were both defensive of our respective emotional positions. So we simply swapped news of our daughters and grandchildren as a couple of friendly, middle aged women might do. It was a strangely inconsequential meeting although we parted promising to stay in touch and I suspect we felt we had done the right thing.

I stayed another couple of days with my friend who I had known for many years. We had both shared a lot of personal history and I felt very comforted by being with her at this time. But the future had to be faced and I had eventually to go home. When I got there I found there were numerous messages from David on my phone and the next day he arrived at my house with all his belongings in the back of his car. He hugged me and told me he realised he was in his words, "giving up the wrong woman" and that I was the woman he loved. But I had changed and although I still loved David and was blissfully happy to fall into his arms there was another me that couldn't just go back to the way things were.

In the name of restoring our relationship we went for a week to Ireland which was a place we had both always loved. It was a strange little holiday, which brought us back together but was underpinned by a kind of unspoken sadness. One day we drove out to Louisburg and walked by the beautiful grey sea, cloaked in Irish mist. On our way back to the car we found an old bungalow with a sign on it for rent. It was set on a narrow plot of land which someone had started to turn over and left a solitary garden spade sticking up in the soil. Both David and I had the simultaneous thought that it was waiting for us and we arranged to view the bungalow. We had always had a dream of selling up and moving to Ireland and thought maybe now was the time to do it. But although I joined in the plan and even arranged a viewing, I knew that I was holding something back in a way that I had never done before.

Before we left Louisburg we visited the Famine Museum which is poorly publicised as the Irish people seem almost ashamed of this part of their past. The writer Nuala O'Faolain, whom we both admired has described the reluctance of the Irish to talk about the Famine in her book "My Dream of You" as the shame of the survivor. David and I talked about this and the fact that earlier that year O'Faolain had made it public that she was choosing to die of her recently diagnosed cancer rather than have treatment. David greatly admired her for that but we were unaware of how significant it was to become.

Perhaps all this was just a fortunate preparation because not long after we came back from Ireland David was also diagnosed with lung cancer and, if I am honest, to my relief we had to cancel our dream. The diagnosis was a terrible blow to both of us but I was able to cope with it because, although I still loved him and had grown close to him again, I also had my newfound, independent inner self. David was also very philosophical about his cancer. He agreed to some treatment but was adamant that he was not going, in his words, "to get involved in the whole cancer thing".

Ironically, we had an amazing final year together which was still full of walking, talking and laughing even though much of it took place in hospital waiting rooms. After a year of fairly successful chemo and just as things looked to be settling down for at least another year, David had two massive epileptic fits which put him in a coma. For a month I sat everyday by his bed in the hospital, reading poems to him and his favourite bits of Joyce's Ulysses. I don't know if he heard them or not but it was for me as much as for him. When they moved him to a hospice I knew the game was up but I was glad to have a last week with him, to talk to him and be strong enough to hold him as he left us.

That said, nothing prepared me for the shock of David's death and the terrible feeling of loss made so much worse by the knowledge that there was absolutely nothing that I could do about it. That, however much I wished for it, I couldn't even just have a cup of tea with him. I was so sad that I could not contemplate let alone construct a future, and the past was a forbidden place, too painful to visit. I confined myself to the present and reduced my life to putting one foot in front of the other. I went for long walks telling myself I was not allowed to go home until I stopped crying and I congratulated myself on getting through at the end of each day. This went on for almost a year until in the Autumn some old friends of ours with whom David and I had shared happy times, invited me to stay for a weekend at their home in Norfolk. As we talked and shared our memories I found to my surprise that the past was not only comforting but joyful as well.

My drive home from Norfolk was wonderful. The day was bright with a clear blue sky and trees shimmering in the reds and golds of autumn. As I drove through the Fenlands the freshly turned fields were so many shades of rich dark brown with purple shadows hovering in the hedgerows. I became drenched in the colours and found myself visiting another time. I remembered that in my felt-making days I had bought two lovely old pure wool, cream blankets along with a box of beautiful coloured dyes that I had never had the courage to use and they were all the colours of this journey home. My head began to fill with ideas and I felt an almost physical force of energy invading my body and my soul. I could not wait to get home and do what I had never dared to do.

Throughout the next week I took scissors and cut up the blankets into big squares. My kitchen began to fill with the smell of wet sheep as tubs of blankets boiled in the dyes on my stove. The creamy white turned to the many colours of my autumn drive across the Fens and a plan for them began to evolve. As it did so I found myself creeping towards that broken place where art, love and sex all come together. I had been stuck in an enduring present but now the past came hurtling to my rescue. I stitched the coloured squares together and scattered appliquéd felt flowers across it. I used my coloured threads and my learnt skills left over from the past to start rebuilding myself as the blanket took shape.

I was seventy years old the year that David died and along with my grief, his dying also made me painfully aware of my own mortality. Suddenly I had a felt knowledge of the inevitable end of things and that my own time was now limited. I have always needed a project, not only to absorb my brain and keep my hands busy but, more importantly to give me a sense of movement, of something still to be achieved. When I was young that need came from a dreaded feeling each morning when I woke up, that the day was an empty black hole before me, and that I was without meaning or shape. I had to fill that black hole by re-inventing myself each day and I did that by doing things. It is the things that I have made that have in turn, made me and making things has become central to my sense of myself.

Now, more than ever I needed something to distract me from the newfound knowledge of my own inevitable end. I looked at my house that was full of all the accumulated stuff of my many projects and I thought about my daughter. As an only child it would one day be her job to clear it all up and what a task it would be, so I made a plan. I decided that my final project would be to empty my house by using all the left over stuff from previous projects to make more lovely things. The plan was that when my inevitable end came my daughter would come into my house and find, not a burden of stuff to be sorted and thrown out but just a pile of lovely things.

The blanket had brought about my recovery from David's death so I continued to make them, telling myself I could only use what materials I could find in my house. There is a famous and wonderful illustration to the fairy story The Princess and the Pea which shows the princess sleeping on a great and various pile of quilts. It is an illustration that has stayed with me and I now hoped to reproduce it with my many blankets. I also discovered that Louise Bourgeois, who was always a role model for me, began in her very old age to make simple experimental textile squares. This was a great release for me, to know that my work with cloth and thread didn't have to always be a useful blanket or quilt but could just be of any size and probably useless, as long as it pleased me and took me somewhere I had never been before. Using up the stuff in my house also applied to my many scribbled notebooks. I started to go through them and use bits to fashion into short stories and I worked on perfecting my poems.

14

Getting it all together

Two or three years after David's death I had a phone call from my genetic sister Anne to say that 'our' mother had died peacefully at the age of ninety three and would I like to come to the funeral. I was very moved by the fact that she had invited me and immediately said that I would go. One of my youthful fantasies had always been to turn up at this mother's funeral. I imagined myself as a mysterious figure, dressed all in black who would throw back her veil and reveal herself to be the long hidden daughter. Faced now with the reality of this fantasy I realized that it would be a bad mistake to go to the funeral. Her daughters and her grandchildren had never met me and I looked so exactly like my mother, their grandmother, in almost every way. What a shock it would be for them all if this replica turned up in the midst of their mourning. Not only would I be a distraction at a very private and emotional time, but also a reminder of something best forgotten at such a moment. I phoned Anne and explained that I would rather not come to the funeral and I suspect she too was a little relieved. A week later she phoned me again and told me that 'my mother' wanted me to have the picture she had painted of Helmsley, the place of my birth and which she had proudly shown me when I last met with her. I said I would arrange to stay with my friend in Somerset again so that we could meet up and I could collect the painting.

We met in the same pub as the last time but it was a very different meeting. Unlike all the other times there was something very real about it. Anne handed over the painting which was wrapped in brown paper and tied with string, and we talked a little but not much. What we did both keep saying was that our meeting felt different this time. We briefly held hands and the touch was more real this time. We looked at each other with different eyes and perhaps saw each other more clearly. We both agreed that now 'our mother' and all her pain no longer stood between us, there was no more anger and no need to be defensive. In a sense we met each other properly for the first time like two adults independent of the past and it felt all right even if it was still fraught with problems. Anne told me how angry she had felt at having been denied the knowledge of me for all those years and that now she felt she had to get used to what she called 'a new normal'. For the first time I took this on board and realized what a lot she had to cope with. For my part I still felt a conflict of loyalties towards what I felt were my own, proper sisters whom I loved as true sisters.

I didn't open up and look at the painting until I got back to my own home. It turned out to be a large oil painting of cottages and the church spire in Helmsley and concentrated on the huddled roofs of the buildings. The cottages were painted from the back showing tiny details of the back gardens and the brook which ran along below them. It was beautifully painted and seemed almost abstract partly because although it was a busy picture there were no people in it all. I saw Mildred had signed the picture in very small letters in the corner and I felt both honored and proud to have it. I hung the picture in the spare bedroom since although I increasingly loved it I couldn't cope with seeing it every day. I do however regularly look at it, enjoy it and hug to myself the sense of maybe sharing a little heritage through our artistic efforts.

When Anne and I parted we both agreed that we still wanted to pursue our relationship, if for no other reason than we shared a full set of genes. So when she told me, a few months later, that she was about to visit an old school friend who lived not far from me I invited her to come and stay with me for the weekend then I could drive her to her friend's. This would be the first time we were to meet in my space and I suddenly became aware that I was not just her sister but the older sister. She had no experience of sisters but I knew what it was like to have a big sister and, much as I loved my big sister, I didn't want that role. However we had a whole weekend to talk and I think to the relief of both of us, agreed that we did not have nor did we want that kind of sister relationship. Our weekend together became not about our relationship but about sharing family history information. I told her how I had discovered from the birth certificates that I was in fact living not far from where our shared mother was born and one of our grandfathers had lived. I took her to see the little terraced house where our mother was born and we shared our amazement that I had come without knowing it, to work in the school almost opposite.

When I first moved from London to the Midlands it took me about three years to find a house and a place I felt I could live in. I looked at so many pretty villages on the fringes of Nottingham and in the beautiful Peak District. But I could never imagine myself being the kind of person that might live in any of them. The house I eventually found, and still live in is half way between the Peak District and the coalfields of North East Derbyshire and is built on a strip of land between a railway and a road that runs between two larger villages. When I first walked into the house I knew immediately that it was the one for me because it had large rooms with high ceilings that reminded me of my old house in London. But it was the view from the front window that sold it to me. It looks out across the road to a wide, open field that stretches as far as the horizon. The field is still farmed and grows barley for the beer trade so the surface is always changing. Although the station has long gone, the trains still run along the back of my house on their way to Sheffield so the place feels very real. However there is no communal space in my village where people might meet and so there is no sense of a community. It has all the joys of living in the countryside but like the city, it provides me with a sense of anonymity that I find both liberating and restful.

It seemed extraordinary to both of us that I should finish up living so close to where my original mother had been born and where one of my grandfather's had lived. Anne told me that she had done quite a bit of research into our family history and she thought that, like a salmon I appeared to have come back to the spawning grounds since much of the family on my mother's side came from this area. And there was yet one more surprise to come. I had decided to take Anne out for our evening meal to a favorite pub of mine. I knew it had good food because it was where I regularly met up for an evening with three of my women friends.

The pub was in a pretty nearby village which was famous for being the home of the Pentrich Martyrs. Apparently in 1817 there had been a revolutionary uprising by a number of stocking knitters, quarrymen and iron workers who determined to march against the government of the times. But they were betrayed and when caught some were exiled to Australia and, as an example three of them were publicly hung. On the wall in the pub there is a large wooden shield that lists the names of the Martyrs in gold. Anne was astonished when she saw this because in her family history research she had found that we were related to one of these martyrs. She pointed out the name of him on the plaque and told me he was something like an uncle many times removed.

So I had not only an ancestor but a rebellious one, however tenuous the link. I was known amongst my family and especially my sisters as a rebellious child. I always wondered where that nature came from and why was mine so different from my more acquiescent sisters. My family thought it was because I was the middle child and apparently they are known to be difficult. I always felt it related to my knowledge of my adopted status. I was definitely not any less loved by my family but I thought maybe it was the knowledge of having been given away. Now it seemed that it might be nature and not nurture after all and I had inherited rebellious genes. This weekend of family history made a huge difference to me and my confidence in myself as a real person. Until now I had been someone whose life had been defined by a sense of having no history along with not quite knowing where I belonged in the scheme of things. Now, suddenly I had ancestors, I had roots, and for the first time in my life, at the age of seventy six I felt legitimate.

Before Anne left she told me that one of her daughters and her grand daughter both of whom were gifted musicians, were performing in a musical evening to be held by their local operatic society. She asked me if I would like to stay with her for that weekend and go to the concert. It would be a chance for me to meet her family all of whom wanted to meet me. Bathed in the confidence of my new legitimate status I didn't hesitate to accept the invite. However, I was to discover that recovery from a life time of insecurity is not to be that easily and quickly achieved. When Anne emailed me saying she had forgotten to mention that it was a 'posh frock' do, all my confidence instantly drained away since I had absolutely no idea of what a 'posh frock' was.

I have never been keen on shopping, especially for clothes but I have always been very careful of the way I dress. I am fearful of creating an image that I will have to perform to or live up to and mostly wear quiet colors, browns, greys and black. I also very much like wearing second hand clothes and if I buy new clothes I often don't wear them for quite a time until they have grown familiar hanging in my wardrobe. Broadly speaking I conform to the style of the day, according to my age since I want to be accepted rather than noticed. But I always just slightly undermine it with a casual touch of eccentricity that says 'don't think you can draw a line round me or that I care what I look like. I am a work in progress'.

The idea of a 'posh frock' sent me into such a total panic that I rang Anne to say that maybe, since it was a family do, it would be better if I didn't go. She was disappointed and wanted me to meet her family so I relented and agreed to go. The next thing I did was phone my sisters to ask them what I should do. My youngest sister sent me a photo of a line up of girls in their prom dresses with the message "I can't quite see you in any of these"!. My eldest sister told me to stop worrying and just wear something safe and smart that I felt comfortable in. I associated the words safe and smart with Marks and Spencer so I went there to look for a dress although I have never thought of myself as an M&S person. As it happened I found a dress that seemed to fill my eldest sister's advice and I tried it on. When I came out of the changing room to look in the long mirror, two women waiting in the queue said how lovely I looked in it. So on their recommendation I bought it, took it home and hung it up on my bedroom door.

As the weeks went by the more I looked at it the dress, the more I came to dislike it and eventually hate it. I tried it on many times and each time the feeling of not being me got worse. In desperation I did the obvious thing, which in my panic I had never thought of. I went to a shop where I had previously found clothes that I liked and would describe as classy but quirky. It was pouring with rain on the day I went so the shop was empty and the young shop assistant was all mine. I told her what the dress was for, including the back story of my going to meet this new family for the first time. She was thrilled by the story saying it was just like a television show and she joined in my search with relish. She was lovely and knew just what I needed. I came away with a plain grey dress in a lovely, expensive looking, soft, grey material but with a dropped waist and a quirky hemline.

With the problem solved I now felt sufficiently confident to go to Anne's and meet her family. I went down on the day of the concert expecting to meet her two daughters and two of her grandchildren to whom I was technically an aunt and a great aunt, at her home. But they were already getting ready at the concert hall so I met them there in my new dress. It was quite a grand affair and when we arrived they were busy laying small tables with gold clothes and tea lights as there was to be an interval with food. They welcomed me with open arms which was really all they could do as we were in the full glare of a public in posh dress. Anne spent most of the evening helping out in the kitchen and her daughter who was not one of the performers took on the role of looking after me.

The music was lovely and Anne's other daughter and grand daughter were very talented musicians. It was not hard to enjoy the evening although I had never been to anything like it before. I was introduced to lots of people as Anne's sister and as people politely commented on how much I looked like her or that they could see the family resemblance, I felt increasingly unreal. I acted out the role and did it well I think, except at one point, and maybe it was just the beauty of the music, I felt so lost and so guilty towards my own sisters that I found myself silently crying. I think it was equally stressful for Anne's daughter who sat with me and did all the introductions because as soon as the concert ended she left for home with a migraine.

I slept badly that night and I to my horror when I woke at around three in the morning I found I had started to wet the bed. Fortunately it was only my pyjamas and not the bed that got wet so I lay on a towel in case it happened again and tried to sleep some more. The next morning we all met again in a pub for breakfast which was quite jolly but essentially their family affair and I kept a very low profile. I did notice that the youngest grand daughter kept looking at me and Anne told me later that she was a little upset because I looked so much like her great grandmother whom she still loved and missed. So it seems that in spite of everything my very presence can still bring unhappiness and although it suited me well, I have never worn that dress again.

A month later my youngest sister came over from Canada where she now lived because we had promised our mother when she died that we would always stay in touch. Every couple of years either my youngest sister would visit or my eldest sister and I would go to Canada. This time she stayed with my eldest sister in Hertfordshire and I went down to join them for the week. On the weekend we arranged for all the family on this side of the Atlantic, our children and grand children, to meet up for a family picnic. Everyone had brought a contribution of food for the picnic and we all had stories to tell as most of the recipes for what we brought came from the mother and great grandmother of us all. It was a day full of sunshine and sixteen of us went for a walk after the picnic. Aunts and cousins, mothers and fathers, sisters and brother-in-laws, fanned out across the late summer fields as we shared family jokes and tried to work out what our relationships were to each other. We all lead very different lives but we were a family and I felt very much a loved part of it. It would seem that nature may be there but nurture is a transcending element.

I have since met up again with my genetic sister Anne and we are both still intent on pursuing our relationship not only in acknowledgement of our genes and the things we increasingly find similar between us but because we also like each other. We both agree that nature is not enough and it is what you do together that counts so that's what we intend to work on. That said, when I was shuffling through old notebooks as part of getting this all together I found a copy of a letter that I wrote back in 1991. At the time I had read an article in a magazine about a number of women who were developing a practice of massaging their breasts and taking hormones so that they could breast feed their adopted babies. I was horrified by the idea which felt almost like cannibalism to me. This is what I wrote and I include it here as I still believe it to be the truth of the matter :

> "For adopted children a mother's milk is too close to blood for comfort. If they are to successfully deal with the problems of love and identity that they will face as they grow up, both they and their parents need to feel that there is nothing 'less' in the adopted relationship. That as parents they do not make their child feel loved by making it as much like a natural birth as possible. They do it by taking on the full identity of that child which includes being adopted".

As well as my brother, I have many friends who were adopted since it is not an uncommon thing these days and we are all more open about it. We have different experiences, some adopted at birth, some later in life, some that worked out well, some more troublesome. But we also all share something, which is our adopted status. It is in the marrow of our bones and an essential part of our identity. We do not have to explain to each other because we know it, in the sense that we have all lived it. For myself, I find that I have always been, and remain most comfortable on the edge of things with a foot in many camps. Now I stay there out of choice and no longer feel a sense of failure if I do not properly belong. At last I live in the luxury of knowing who I am but it took a long time to find out, almost a lifetime.

Lightning Source UK Ltd.
Milton Keynes UK
UKHW03f2202050418
320585UK00002B/121/P